**New Directions for
Student Services**

Elizabeth J. Whitt
EDITOR-IN-CHIEF

John H. Schuh
ASSOCIATE EDITOR

Creating Successful Multicultural Initiatives in Higher Education and Student Affairs

Sherry K. Watt
Jodi L. Linley
EDITORS

Number 144 • Winter 2013
Jossey-Bass
San Francisco

CREATING SUCCESSFUL MULTICULTURAL INITIATIVES IN HIGHER EDUCATION
AND STUDENT AFFAIRS
Sherry K. Watt, Jodi L. Linley (eds.)
New Directions for Student Services, no. 144

Elizabeth J. Whitt, Editor-in-Chief
John H. Schuh, Associate Editor

NEW DIRECTIONS FOR STUDENT SERVICES (ISSN 0164-7970, e-ISSN 1536-
0695) is part of The Jossey-Bass Higher and Adult Education Series and
is published quarterly by Wiley Subscription Services, Inc., A Wiley Company, at Jossey-Bass, One Montgomery Street, Suite 1200, San Francisco,
CA 94104-4594. POSTMASTER: Send address changes to New Directions
for Student Services, Jossey-Bass, One Montgomery Street, Suite 1200,
San Francisco, CA 94104-4594.

New Directions for Student Services is indexed in CIJE: Current Index to
Journals in Education (ERIC), Contents Pages in Education (T&F), Current Abstracts (EBSCO), Education Index /Abstracts (H.W. Wilson), Educational Research Abstracts Online (T&F), ERIC Database (Education
Resources Information Center), and Higher Education Abstracts (Clare-
mont Graduate University).

Microfilm copies of issues and articles are available in 16 mm and 35 mm,
as well as microfiche in 105mm, through University Microfilms Inc., 300
North Zeeb Road, Ann Arbor, Michigan 48106-1346.

SUBSCRIPTIONS cost $89 for individuals in the U.S., Canada, and Mexico,
and $113 in the rest of the world for print only; $89 in all regions for
electronic only; and $98 in the U.S., Canada, and Mexico for combined
print and electronic; and $122 for combined print and electronic in the
rest of the world. Institutional print only subscriptions are $311 in the
U.S., $351 in Canada and Mexico, and $385 in the rest of the world; electronic only subscriptions are $311 in all regions; and combined print and
electronic subscriptions are $357 in the U.S., $397 in Canada and Mexico,
and $431 in the rest of the world.

EDITORIAL CORRESPONDENCE should be sent to the Editor-in-Chief,
Elizabeth J. Whitt, University of California Merced, 5200 North Lake Rd.
Merced, CA 95343.

www.josseybass.com

Contents

EDITORS' NOTES

This volume provides college educators (higher education administrators, student affairs professionals, and faculty) with guiding principles for the design and implementation of successful multicultural initiatives. A *multicultural initiative* is any type of program and/or a set of strategies that promotes skill development to better manage difference on a personal, institutional, community, or societal level. College educators aim to prepare students to function successfully in an increasingly diverse world. In order for our society to sustain itself, it is necessary that we prepare college students to engage with difference in ways that are productive. *Difference* is having dissimilar opinions, experiences, ideologies, epistemologies, and/or constructions of reality about self, society, and/or identity.

Institutions of higher education have come to understand the value of providing diverse experiences for college students (Pascarella, Edison, Nora, Hagedorn, and Terenzini, 1996). Recently, Haring-Smith (2012) has gone one step further and pointed out that when there is homogeneity in experiences, beliefs, and aspirations in an environment then student learning suffers. For over thirty years, institutions of higher education have sought to become inclusive environments where difference is valued and students learn to become effective global citizens (Pascarella, Edison, Nora, Hagedorn, and Terenzini, 1996). Some multicultural initiatives have thrived while others have flailed, and only recently have scholars begun to reflect on and study various initiatives.

This volume is a resource for those who are looking for practical tips on designing and implementing successful multicultural initiatives. By sharing concrete examples of multicultural initiatives, the authors in this volume are inviting readers into a conversation that might spark change or a new initiative on the reader's own campus.

The underlying assumptions for this volume are as follows:

1. Post-secondary education, in part, fosters good citizens by equipping them with the skills to manage difference.
2. Opportunities for skill development to better manage difference need to be provided at multiple levels of the organization, including campus-wide, the unit level, and discipline or department level.
3. College educators (higher education administrators, student affairs professionals, and faculty) need to work together to provide seamless experiences to support the development of students as good citizens.
4. Engaging students in multicultural initiatives is the responsibility of all college educators regardless of their role on campus or their personal identity (for example, race, sexual orientation, political orientation, ability, or gender).

New Directions for Student Services, no. 144, Winter 2013 © 2013 Wiley Periodicals, Inc.
Published online in Wiley Online Library (wileyonlinelibrary.com) • DOI: 10.1002/ss.20063

5. Successful implementation of multilevel transformational approaches to multicultural initiatives carries over into the classroom which highlights the need for faculty involvement.
6. College educators are continuously learning and developing their own skills for managing difference, in addition to providing opportunities for students to do the same.
7. All multicultural initiatives are projects being implemented within a dynamic cultural context. While there are guiding principles that increase the likelihood of program success, there can be no flawless multicultural initiatives due to the ever-changing nature of people and organizations.

This volume (1) introduces "diversity as a value versus diversity as a good" as a conceptual lens through which to view multicultural initiatives, (2) presents useful guidelines as well as (3) programmatic examples that will help college educators design and implement multicultural initiatives on their own campuses. Analyzing initiatives through the conceptual lens discussed in Chapter 1 (diversity as a value versus diversity as a good) will assist educators in identifying the philosophical foundation of a given initiative. For example, college educators can ask themselves the fundamental question—*is their multicultural initiative grounded in surface-level outcomes or in far-reaching change?* Readers, including practitioners, administrators, and faculty, will have examples of programs from the full spectrum of the value–good conceptual frame.

This volume highlights the approaches various campus leaders take to design and implement successful multicultural initiatives. On the whole, this volume presents different types of initiatives across *various settings* (campus-wide, STEM support programs, student affairs programs, small private campuses, larger public campuses, and approaches across classroom settings) implemented by *various educators* (faculty, senior administrators, student affairs staff, graduate students, and social change agents outside the institution). The chapters also describe a variety of *target audiences*, including undergraduates (student staff, students enrolled in specific courses, student volunteers, and students majoring in specific disciplines), master's students enrolled in a required multiculturalism course, and administrators within a division of student affairs. In general, Chapters 1 and 2 provide overarching practical ideas whereas Chapters 3–10 offer examples from a variety of large, public universities and one private institution. These examples represent multicultural initiatives at varying levels of institutions, from central administration to specific units.

In Chapter 1, Watt provides a *conceptual lens* as well as *guiding principles* for designing and implementing successful multicultural initiatives. In Chapter 2, Elkins, Morris, and Schimek clarify the importance and uses of *assessment* in multicultural initiatives. These authors provide clear examples of its utility on a small, liberal arts campus.

In Chapters 3–7, the authors explore multicultural initiatives that are broad-based. Dodge and Jarratt analyze a *comprehensive, campus-wide* multicultural initiative in Chapter 3. Their initiative—a campus affiliate of the National Coalition Building Institute—is on a large, public, predominantly white university campus. The multicultural initiative explored by Pasquesi in Chapter 4 is from the same university, but its focus is *course-based undergraduate service learning.* Students seeking social justice oriented courses are the target population of the multicultural initiative described in Chapter 5 as well. In this chapter, Arbisi-Kelm, Clay, Lin, Horikawa, Clifton, and Kapani detail a *grass-roots social justice course* and its outcomes for undergraduate participants and facilitators, along with curricular examples. Master's students preparing for careers in higher education and student affairs are the target group of the *graduate multiculturalism course* described in Chapter 6. Watt, Golden, Schumacher, and Moreno discuss the use of the Principles and Practices of the Circles of Trust® approach when facilitating a course as a multicultural initiative and share an example of a class activity. Undergraduates are the participants in the initiative explored in Chapter 7, but these students were selected for competitive leadership positions and are required to participate in the initiative. In this chapter, Petryk, Thompson, and Boynton share examples from a large *housing system's training course.*

Chapters 8–10 describe multicultural initiatives that are intentionally not comprehensive. All of the initiatives in these final chapters were designed to address specific issues. In Chapter 8, Obear and martinez discuss the use of *race caucuses* as professional development in response to issues of racism in a division of student affairs. In Chapter 9, Hicks and Tran-Parsons examine two initiatives designed to foster *spiritual development and interfaith engagement* at a Jesuit, Catholic institution in an urban setting and a large, public, metropolitan university. Both initiatives were developed in response to President Barack Obama's Interfaith and Community Service Challenge. In Chapter 10, Linley and George-Jackson wrestle with the design of *undergraduate programs for underrepresented students in science, technology, engineering, and math* (STEM) as multicultural initiatives. These initiatives have been created as attempts to increase the number of people of color and women in STEM fields.

Sherry K. Watt
Jodi L. Linley
Editors

References

Haring-Smith, T. "Broadening Our Definition of Diversity." *Liberal Education,* 2012, 98(2), 6–13.

Pascarella, E. T., Edison, M., Nora, A., Hagedorn, L. S., and Terenzini, P. T. "Influences on Students' Openness to Diversity and Challenge in the First Year of College." *Journal of Higher Education*, 1996, 67(2), 174–195.

SHERRY K. WATT *is an associate professor of higher education and student affairs at the University of Iowa. Her research on privileged identity exploration expands the understanding of the various ways in which people react to difficult dialogue.*

JODI L. LINLEY *is a doctoral student of higher, adult, and lifelong education at Michigan State University, with a longstanding career and research agenda centered on issues of equity and multiculturalism.*

1

This chapter provides guiding principles for designing and implementing successful multicultural initiatives. A rationale for why these elements transcend both higher education and student affairs settings is presented. In addition to providing guiding principles, this chapter includes advice for socially and politically conscious-minded professionals who are leading the implementation of multicultural initiatives on their campus.

Designing and Implementing Multicultural Initiatives: Guiding Principles

Sherry K. Watt

I will be preparing your arrival
as a gardener tends to the garden
for those that shall come in the spring.
Paulo Freire, Obvious Song (Freire, 2004, p. xxviii)

Many student affairs professionals and higher education administrators are drawn to college environments because they are gardeners of a sort. These professionals view their work as if they are tending to a garden where they plant seeds, fertilize the soil, and facilitate the growth of the people and the organization. Paulo Freire's metaphor in his poem *Obvious Song* may resonate with those practitioners who see their institution as having ever-evolving plants that come in the form of people (students, faculty, staff, and administrators) and environments (organizational and administrative structures) all existing within an increasingly diverse world. In this diverse world, communities manage the historical tensions between those marginalized and classically privileged groups. Systemic oppression describes the relationship between "embedded, integrated, and interacting contexts and social roles" (Cecero, 2010, p. 498). Systemic oppression frames the way that privileged and marginalized groups exist and interact in society. It results in unhealthy organizations and damaged relationships between members of the community. As Lewin's (1936) Behavior = Function (Person × Environment) classic equation points out, our hope is that if we plant seeds that support the development of *people* and fertilize a healthy organization, then people in the *environment* will learn to *behave* as good

New Directions for Student Services, no. 144, Winter 2013 © 2013 Wiley Periodicals, Inc.
Published online in Wiley Online Library (wileyonlinelibrary.com) • DOI: 10.1002/ss.20064

citizens who advance worthy causes in the world, which is the desired behavioral outcome (Huebner and Lawson, 1990).

The National Task Force on Civic Learning and Democratic Engagement (2012) states that beyond economic prosperity the larger purpose of education is to engage its citizens civically, intellectually, morally, and ethically. In order for education to fulfill its purpose, it is necessary that we prepare college students to engage with difference in ways that are productive. *Difference* is having dissimilar opinions, experiences, ideologies, epistemologies, and/or constructions of reality about self, society, and/or identity. How well one manages conflict related to *Difference* is an essential skill set for living in diverse societies. For example, a first-year college student raised in one religious value system is likely going to encounter another student from a different faith tradition and each may differ on how they view certain issues, such as the role of males versus females in the home, contraception/birth control, or abortion/right to life. Part of the college experience is to engage in dialogue with others who have different views. Through high-impact experiences inside and outside the classroom, educators aim to increase students' knowledge, skills, and awareness (Pope, Reynolds, and Mueller, 2004) related to both their discipline of study and also these types of differences.

Whether student affairs professionals and higher education administrators are designing programs to facilitate personal development or working to set up organizational structures to create effective learning environments, it all works together toward the ultimate goal, which is to provide college students with a holistic education that will prepare them to function as good citizens in society.

What does it mean to be a good citizen? Ravitch and Viteritti (2001) criticize the role of education in "instilling or nourishing the values that form a disposition toward responsible citizenship" (p. 6) due to educator's fear of controversy. Ravitch and Viteritti allude to the characteristics of a good citizen by referring to a person's ability to handle important ethical questions and engage in highly nuanced discussions "that require knowledge and involved crucial moral considerations, so as to engage in principled debates" (p. 6). This chapter assumes that good citizens not only are engaged in their community but also have personally developed the skills to interact in meaningful and responsible ways around difference (people, ideas, identities, experiences, and so on). This important skill set helps college students be active agents in change around social and political issues.

The Boyer Commission on Educating Undergraduates in the Research University (1995) posits that higher education institutions should cultivate the mind, abilities, and talents of college students toward them becoming productive and responsible citizens. The Boyer Commission suggests all institutions should offer a student careful and comprehensive preparation for postgraduate work, a wide range of quality opportunities to study the arts, humanities, sciences, and social sciences, as well as opportunities to learn

NEW DIRECTIONS FOR STUDENT SERVICES • DOI: 10.1002/ss

through thinking critically rather than just the transmission of knowledge. Going even further, the Boyer Commission calls on research institutions to extend beyond those basic criteria and offer not only first-class facilities but also expanded opportunities to research and "opportunities to interact with people of backgrounds, cultures, and experiences different from the student's own and with pursuers of knowledge at every level of accomplishment, from freshmen students to senior research faculty" (p. 13). Among these maximal opportunities for creative and intellectual development, the Boyer Commission has identified that a key element of learning is how to engage effectively with difference as essential for the development of good citizens.

We are living in socially turbulent times. There is push back against the dominant paradigms that are more evident on college campuses than any other environment. For example, college students today are questioning binary references to male and female, uses of heterosexist language, and biases toward structural racism. College educators have to wrestle with complex questions prompted by campus community members requiring gender-inclusive restrooms, the rights of undocumented students who have lived in this country since grade school, and a disproportionate number of white male and female faculty and administrators. The tensions between the dominant and subordinate paradigm are heightening. College campuses are microcosms of our larger society. It is the responsibility of administrators, faculty, and staff on college campuses to create an environment where these complex issues are handled well and represent good examples of how to exist in a diverse society.

Many institutions attempt to encourage skill development for managing *Difference* by designing various types of multicultural initiatives. A *multicultural initiative* is any type of program and/or a set of strategies that promote skill development to better manage difference on a personal, institutional, community, or societal level. The basic premise behind this chapter is that developing multicultural initiatives that promote skill development for managing *Difference* influences social change. And working toward positive and inclusive social change is every campus community member's responsibility. It is necessary that college campuses create a culture whereby faculty, administrators, staff, and students skillfully manage controversy related to social and political issues. College campuses should be places where campus community members foster an environment where healthy interaction around controversy is nurtured. Healthy interaction around controversy requires a disposition where difference is engaged, not judged to be bad or good. In other words, healthy engagement with *Difference* allows for an acknowledgment that there are valid differences in belief systems and each must engage in the exploration of other ideas while withholding judgment.

The purpose of this chapter is to introduce a few of the basic principles for designing and implementing multicultural initiatives across student

NEW DIRECTIONS FOR STUDENT SERVICES • DOI: 10.1002/ss

affairs and higher education settings. To begin, I introduce a conceptual lens through which to view diversity efforts in higher educational settings. Second, I outline guiding principles for designing effective multicultural initiatives. Lastly, I share advice for college educators who are taking on leadership roles in the design and implementation of these types of campus initiatives.

Diversity as a "Social Value" versus Diversity as a "Social Good"

There are many definitions of diversity. Diversity as defined in the Editors' Notes is *the state of having difference*. A multicultural initiative aims to help campus community members understand and better navigate *Difference*. Prior to designing a multicultural initiative, a college educator must assess the intentions behind their multicultural initiative as it relates to diversity. The leaders of these types of initiatives will have to decide if the purpose of their program or set of strategies is aimed toward diversity as a social "value" or as a social "good" (Watt, 2011). In other words, is your intention through this program or set of strategies to change the culture and the fundamental ways *Difference* is managed on campus? Or is your initiative aiming to create space for the "marginalized or historically traumatized" (Kaleem, 2012, "Specialized Retreats," para. 2) to exist on campus? Campus community members asking questions guided by this conceptual frame can more purposefully align their goals for an inclusion effort on their campus with the intended outcome.

Principally, "diversity as a social good" requires a surface level commitment to systemic change with a focus on outcomes without attempting to assess or dismantle the underlying problems that contribute to marginalization. An initiative operating off of this underlying assumption primarily and simply operates within the larger societal systemic structure, and the programs or strategies do not make attempts to drastically change the mode of functioning. Inclusion efforts viewed through this lens will meet the basic guidelines of state or federal law in that they require inclusion of those individuals who have been historically marginalized, but these efforts do very little to change the dominant culture influence and the traditional ways the campus operates. In other words, these inclusion efforts are led primarily by those in marginalized groups, they address relegated experiences on campus, and they occur outside of and/or in addition to the mainstream campus agenda. For example, a large predominantly white campus community hires a director of multicultural programs whose primary responsibility is to provide support to the students of color on campus. This director designs and implements programs, such as Black Alumni Reunion, or hosts social programs at the black cultural center targeted primarily at black students. These activities are held in conjunction with or in addition to other mainstream large campus events, such as major sporting events. Viewing inclusion efforts through the lens of "diversity as a social good" has pros and cons. This director of multicultural programs position is dedicated to providing support to a group of students that is in the minority on campus and all students need to find a community when coming to campus. For many black students, this focused attention and intentional community could be a benefit. And yet, the structure of the position is such that the culture of the campus will not change and the skill development for engaging with differences is more likely to occur for the small number of black students and not the predominant number of white students on campus. Further, the intention of this inclusion effort is really to operate within the cultural norms that focus on the individual and continue to perpetuate a divide between marginalized and privileged groups.

Essentially, a multicultural initiative structured for "diversity as a social value" embraces strategies to disrupt systematic oppression on a deeper level with a shift toward considering diversity matters as "a central and integrative dimension rather than required and marginalized" (Watt, 2011, p. 132). A multicultural initiative that holds "diversity as a social value" fundamentally questions the underlying structures that bind the way campus community members interact. In other words, the focus is on the system and not on the individual's position in the system. An initiative that operates from this value system considers the historical, social, and political context and engages in systemic analysis across all of those levels. Also, this cross-level analysis couples thoughtful dialogue with bold and innovative action. Lastly, when an initiative holds this social value, the work toward social change is shared across those who are historically marginalized and privileged. Further, the effort to create a culture change with this initiative is led by high-level campus administrators such as vice presidents, presidents, department chair, and deans. For example, an inclusion effort in an academic program that embraces diversity as a value would be led by a department chair or a senior faculty member. This inclusion effort might focus on creating a culture where students of color and diversity initiatives are not just tolerated, but made a central focus of the work done in the department. This could take the form of the department chair leading the faculty members to work together to create a culture both inside and outside of the classroom where *Difference* is engaged. This could be not only "what" we discuss within community but also "how" we discuss it. For instance, engaging *Difference* could involve creating more opportunities for thoughtful reflection and dialogue on the academic content and its connection to or divergence from *Difference*. It might also involve treating differences of opinions or experiences as chances to engage ideas and consider that a positive way of interacting within the community. If the faculty led by example, then this practice of engaging *Difference* as a positive practice would become a community value. Intentional and conscious action can be taken to question the traditional practices and conduct cross-level analysis from both a historical and a sociopolitical lens. Specifically, a program that embraces diversity as a social value does not only focus on making difference

NEW DIRECTIONS FOR STUDENT SERVICES • DOI: 10.1002/ss

(that is, multicultural curricula content, domestic students of color, sexual minorities, and international students) welcomed once "it" arrives but also leads efforts to intentionally change "how things are done here." A program or set of strategies that embraces this value is evidenced when *Difference* is affirmed and there is an intentional shift in the culture to centralize and/or balance marginalized ideas and experiences with dominant ones.

There are pros and cons to approaching inclusion efforts with the philosophy of diversity as a value. Beginning with a con, this requires that the leadership of an academic department makes a decision to have intentional synergy around meaningful diversity work as a central program value. This approach requires relationship building, which is an investment in time and personal as well as professional energy. Engaging *Difference* in this way can bring about feelings of resistance that can manifest in how people react and receive this cultural shift. On a positive note, engaging in the process of a cultural shift that nurtures an environment where *Difference* is managed proactively has the potential to put academic programs slightly ahead of the inevitable changes that are occurring due to demographic shifts in this country.

It is necessary that campus community members not only consciously consider what operating principle underlie their multicultural initiatives but also understand the guiding principles that should inform their efforts when aiming to increase skill development with managing *Difference*.

Three Guiding Principles for Designing Effective Multicultural Initiatives

The basic principles of an effective multicultural initiative assume that the development of the skills to effectively manage *Difference* requires *a multilevel transformational approach* involving individual and community, institutional and societal, and policy and attitudes. Sustainable approaches to managing *Difference* on multiple levels require dialogue and action that *balances the head* (intellect/thought), *heart* (emotion/spirit), *and hands* (practical/real-world application) (Potapchuk, Leiderman, Bivens, and Major, 2005). Lastly, an effective multicultural initiative requires careful and thoughtful planning to *align the goals with the outcomes*.

Multilevel Transformational Approach. Engaging *Difference* in healthy ways involves systemic-level shifts within social structures/institutions, attitudes, practices, and thoughts as well as policies and procedures that guide how citizens relate to each other within a community. A multilevel transformational approach aims to evidence these types of systemic-level shifts in the behaviors of its community members. It is the hope that healthy engagement with *Difference* will influence positive social change efforts. Social change involves acts of advocacy among individuals with shared values to transform their community in normative ways (Haferkamp and Smelser, 1992). Practicing a multilevel transformational approach within a campus community requires seamless interaction between higher education administration and student affairs. Campus administrators who embrace this approach understand that substantive organizational change comes about when they are employing multilevel strategies. These multilevel strategies are not hinged on a particular professional identity; rather it calls for all college educators (staff, student affairs practitioners, faculty, and administrators) to work together using their skills and resources to take action to disrupt the structural inequities that historically have limited the experiences of marginalized groups while privileging the experiences of others.

For example, if a campus community aims to discourage hate crimes, then the campus must initiate a multilevel approach that addresses the campus culture by revisiting the policies and procedures both spoken and unspoken. In other words, campus leaders must not only consider the acknowledged policies and procedures for sanctions for undesirable behavior, and the guidelines for who is included and who is not in the campus activities groups, but also examine the more subtle practices for how *Difference* is treated and what the expectations are for how members should interact with each other when they disagree.

A campus administrator whose multicultural initiatives are guided by this multilevel approach can define their goals and objectives by devising a comprehensive plan that employs a program or set of strategies that addresses individual and community, institutional and societal, and policy and attitude levels. Within each of these levels, an effective multicultural initiative engages its campus community members by inviting individuals (1) to intellectually explore what it means to engage *Difference*, (2) to emotionally examine how engaging with *Difference* impacts their individual and collective behavior, and (3) finally, to consider ways they might take action to increase their capacity for managing *Difference* not only as individuals but also as a community.

Balancing Head, Heart, and Hands. *Community change strategies that are lasting need to include skill development that balances the head* (intellect/thought), *heart* (emotion/spirit), *and hands* (practical/real-world application) (Potapchuk, Leiderman, Bivens, and Major, 2005). Campus leaders have to use their intellect to take a wide view of the historical and sociopolitical context as well as examine the scholarly literature that helps to inform their view of the challenges they are facing. While campus leaders can think through the challenges they are facing in this way, it is also necessary when engaging a multilevel approach that they also locate emotionally where personal values and beliefs associated with the changes fit. Lastly, this approach requires that what you think, feel, and learn is all brought to bear on what you do. For instance, our culture is structured around "racist thought, emotion, and action" (Feagin, 2010, p. 10), and that trifecta results in a system that limits the lives of people of color and advantages white people. It is counterproductive and unbalanced to design a multicultural initiative that only addresses one aspect. Considering that structural racism inherently involves aspects of the head, heart, and hands, multicultural initiatives that include this balanced approach require engagement of intellect and emotions that are all applied in some practical way in the community. Multicultural initiatives that do this are the most effective vehicles for facilitating learning that actually result in better skill development for managing *Difference*. As discussed, when designing a multicultural initiative, it is important to address oppression at multiple levels and balance the head, heart, and hands. It is also critically important that the intention for the initiative aligns with the intended outcomes.

Intentional Goal Alignment. When college educators consider whether or not their goal aligns with the intended outcomes of the program or set of strategies, it increases the likelihood that skill development for managing *Difference* will increase. The intent and the purpose of *a multicultural initiative* need to align with its stated goals and outcomes. Many multicultural initiatives have far-reaching goals. As campus leaders with good intentions, we want to change the world to be a better place and intend to start with our own campus community. When a multicultural initiative aims to abstractly and broadly change the world, it is difficult to measure or actualize that goal for many reasons. For instance, changing the world is ill-defined and it could mean many different things to any campus community member. Rather than focusing on lofty goals, campus leaders need to select more actionable goals and employ specific strategies to expand the campus community's capacity to develop skills to better manage *Difference*. Campus leaders who design multicultural initiatives with the goal of teaching the campus community how to think together effectively, how to manage *Difference* and controversy in productive and meaningful ways, and then how to take thoughtful action on their campus after they have examined the history, the sociopolitical context, their personal thoughts, beliefs, and values may or may not immediately change the world. However, this approach may align the program's objectives with more actionable outcomes.

In summary, the above sections review some important guiding principles for campus community members to consider when designing and implementing effective multicultural initiatives. In addition, I introduced the "diversity as a good versus as a value" conceptual lens through which to view diversity efforts in higher educational settings. Finally, in what follows, I share some advice for campus community members who design and facilitate multicultural initiatives in higher education.

Advice for Gardeners: Self-Care and the Socially and Politically Conscious-Minded College Educator

> My body burned by the sun, I will drench it in sweat;
> my hands will become calloused hands,

NEW DIRECTIONS FOR STUDENT SERVICES • DOI: 10.1002/ss

my feet will learn the mystery of the paths
my ears will hear more,
my eyes will see what they did not see before,
while I am waiting for you.
            Paulo Freire, *Obvious Song* (Freire, 2004, p. xxvii)

Paulo Freire's *Obvious Song* reveals how seeding and reseeding our gardens in higher education is not easy work. Many college educators find it challenging to create campus environments where students develop better skills for managing *Difference*. After all, these skills are a sign that they are growing into being good citizens. Throughout the years, I have designed and implemented multicultural initiatives to engage students, faculty, and staff in learning more about themselves and to be thoughtful about their reactions to *Difference*. It is my hope that these opportunities for deep self-reflection nurture a skill that individuals use as they participate in social change efforts. I believe that critical reflection can inform action and profoundly improve the decisions made that impact a community. And while guiding people through this process of critical reflection can be life-affirming and exhilarating, it can also be depleting and disillusioning.

To attend to my angst as I guide individuals, organizations, and communities through this dynamic process, I conduct research that explores reactions individuals have to difficult dialogues. In addition, I am constantly in thoughtful reflection about my experience as a guide/teacher with others. I have learned some helpful lessons through the interplay of my research and experience. In the following, I share three of those lessons:

1. *Focusing Inward Not Outward.* Remember that the journey toward engaging with *Difference* is an inward one. An inward journey is a process by which individuals make observations of their personal reactions to *Difference*. In this process, individuals face their feelings and thoughts about differences as they hold these ideas up against their own values, beliefs, and experiences. An outward journey is a process where others place a defined value on the difference as well as the certain values, beliefs, and experiences, and decide there is a desired reaction. I take the inward journey along with those I guide. Also, I emphasize that this is indeed an inward journey for everyone and it is counterproductive to try to live up to anyone else's expectations in these types of learning experiences. I trust the capacity of everyone to use the critical process I teach as they are ready and to find their own answers.
2. *Partnering and Scheduling Opportunities for Renewal and Reflection.* Whether I am teaching a course, or designing a workshop or a campus-wide initiative, I rarely lead multicultural initiatives solo. These partnerships are necessary for my own sanity. I also believe it is important to give participants in these experiences alternate sources of support. I believe these partnerships help me to be a cleaner, more

NEW DIRECTIONS FOR STUDENT SERVICES • DOI: 10.1002/ss

focused conduit when facilitating controversial discussion. I have also become keenly aware of how important it is to find ways to renew my energy when guiding multicultural initiatives. For me, this might include going for a walk or taking some time to rest and read, and/or going to a multiday retreat.

3. *Managing Defensive Reactions.* My observation of behavior through my research has revealed some useful insights for me (Watt, 2007, 2011). As individuals engage in difficult dialogues about *Difference*, they often initially respond in defensive ways. I have learned that it is helpful to understand as a facilitator that initial responses to dialogue about *Difference* might include reactions, such as denial, rationalization, or intellectualization. Many of these behaviors are launched as a protection in dialogue and are normal reactions to feelings of being threatened. When I see these defensive reactions, I have reacted in ways that have both furthered and hindered the progress toward developing better skills for managing *Difference*. When I facilitate, I try as often as possible to begin by identifying my own reaction to the defensive response from another. Doing this self-assessment creates a space that allows me to more thoughtfully hear another's responses so that I can respond with intention rather than haphazardly.

In closing, I hope that these lessons learned might help college educators who design multicultural initiatives to find respite as they do the difficult work of creating more spaces for effectively engaging with others around *Difference*. It is my hope that facilitators, whether administrators, faculty, staff, or students, can intermittently sit in some shade while they work on the garden that hopefully will produce responsible citizens who can effectively manage controversy (a spring of sorts):

> I chose the shade of this tree
> to rest from all I will do
> while I am waiting for you.
>
> Paulo Freire, *Obvious Song* (Freire, 2004, p. xxvii)

Conclusion

This chapter introduces some basic principles for designing and implementing effective multicultural initiatives that educators can use to critically assess multilevel efforts aimed at engaging campus constituents around *Difference*. And above all, higher education administrators, faculty, and student affairs professionals must understand that better decisions are made for all involved when intentional effort is given to balancing the head, heart, and the hands when engaging *Difference*—whether doing so in the classroom, in campus programming, or as it relates to administrative policy decisions.

New Directions for Student Services • DOI: 10.1002/ss

References

Boyer Commission on Educating Undergraduates in the Research University. *Reinventing Undergraduate Education: A Blueprint for America's Research Universities*, 1995. Retrieved February 17, 2013, from http://www.niu.edu /engagedlearning/research/pdfs/Boyer_Report.pdf

Cecero, J. J. "The Spiritual Exercises in Counseling and Therapy." In J. G. Ponterotto, J. Manual Cases, L. A. Suzuki, and C. A. Alexander (eds.), *Handbook of Multicultural Counseling*. 3rd ed., pp. 479–501. Los Angeles: Sage, 2010.

Feagin, J. *Racist America: Roots, Current Realities and Future Reparations*. 2nd ed. New York: Routledge, 2010.

Freire, P. *Pedagogy of Indignation*. Series in Critical Narratives, edited by D. Macedo. Boulder, Colo.: Paradigm Publishers, 2004.

Haferkamp, H., and Smelser, N. J. (eds.). *Social Change and Modernity*. Berkeley: University of California Press, 1992.

Huebner, L. A., and Lawson, J. M. "Understanding and Assessing College Environments." In D. G. Creamer and Associates (eds.), *College Student Development: Theory and Practice for the 1990's*, pp. 127–154. Alexandria, Va.: American College Personnel Association, 1990.

Kaleem, J. *Buddhist 'People Of Color Sanghas,' Diversity Efforts Address Conflicts About Race Among Meditators*, 2012, November 18. Retrieved March 2, 2013, from http://www.huffingtonpost.com/2012/11/18/buddhism-race-mediators-people -of-color-sangha_n_2144559.html

Lewin, K. *Principles of Topological Psychology*. New York: McGraw-Hill, 1936.

National Task Force on Civic Learning and Democratic Engagement. *A Crucible Moment: College Learning and Democracy's Future*. Washington, D.C.: Association of American Colleges and Universities, 2012.

Pope, R. L., Reynolds, A. L., and Mueller, J. A. *Multicultural Competence in Student Affairs*. San Francisco: Jossey-Bass, 2004.

Potapchuk, M., Leiderman, S., Bivens, D., and Major, B. *Flipping the Script: White Privilege and Community Building*. Silver Springs, Md.: MP Associates, Inc., and the Center for Assessment and Policy Development (CAPD), 2005.

Ravitch, D., and Viteritti, J. P. *Making Good Citizens: Education and Civil Society*. Binghampton, N.Y.: Yale University, 2001.

Watt, S. K. "Developing Cultural Competence: Facilitating Privileged Identity Exploration in Student Affairs Practice." *College Student Affairs Journal 2007 Special Issue*, 2007, *26*(2), 114–126.

Watt, S. K. "Moving Beyond the Talk: From Difficult Dialogues to Action." In J. Armino, V. Torres, and R. Pope. *Why Aren't We There Yet: Taking Personal Responsibility for Creating an Inclusive Campus*. Sterling, Va.: Stylus Publishing, 2011.

SHERRY K. WATT is an associate professor of higher education and student affairs at the University of Iowa. Her research on privileged identity exploration expands the understanding of the various ways in which people react to difficult dialogue.

New Directions for Student Services • DOI: 10.1002/ss

2

This chapter discusses assessment and evaluation of multicultural initiatives by exploring two efforts implemented at a small, liberal arts college.

Making Meaning through Multicultural Initiatives

Becki Elkins, Kenneth Morris, Jr., Gwendolyn Schimek

Baseball season was getting under way in Florida in early spring 2007. A team from a small Midwestern college was at bat. The pitch. The call. "Strike three, you're out!" Outraged, the batter turned to walk back to the dugout, in the process calling the umpire a "fucking nigger." The coach, in disbelief, benched the player for the rest of the game and, on returning to campus, notified the Athletic Director of the incident. The batter, coach, and Athletic Director were all white; the umpire was African American. Weeks passed as administrators across campus, all of whom were white, waited on one another to take the lead in investigating and addressing the situation. With intense pressure by students and the Director of Intercultural Life, the Division of Student Affairs initiated an investigation a month after the incident. The late response, regardless of intent, communicated a lack of concern for the psychological well-being of students of color and placed faculty and staff of color in the precarious position of having to help students while also dealing with their own feelings of anger, disappointment, and marginalization. The "baseball incident," as it came to be known, revealed a lack of administrative transparency and highlighted "privilege" as it emerged in individual roles and group conversations. These discussions were challenging because they illustrated how members of different identity groups experienced the college, this particular incident, and access to power and privilege. They disrupted the image of a post-racial community held by many. As the college moved forward, though, staff, faculty, and students began to attend to target and agent identities and the roles each played in campus conversations, setting the stage for the college to engage in difficult dialogues.

A few years later at this same institution, a study on student persistence by race was conducted (Elkins, 2008). For the years included in the study, students of color comprised, on average, 10 percent of the population. Data revealed that, although first-to-second-year retention rates were similar for

New Directions for Student Services, no. 144, Winter 2013 © 2013 Wiley Periodicals, Inc.
Published online in Wiley Online Library (wileyonlinelibrary.com) • DOI: 10.1002/ss.20065

students of color and white students, only one out of two students of color graduated from the college within six years whereas two out of three white students graduated. Furthermore, on average, one out of three students of color withdrew from the college compared with one out of four white students. The study acknowledged the limitations of small sample sizes and offered questions for consideration, including why, although being retained to the second year, fewer students of color were graduating. Reactions to the study included attempts to dismiss the results as "too small to be meaningful." The Office of Intercultural Life (ICL), however, recognized that this evidence pointed to a need to disrupt the pattern of withdrawals among students of color. Exploring this question with students of color revealed a lack of connection to the institution.

Both events took place at a residential, liberal arts college whose mission encompasses liberal education. Such education "empowers individuals and prepares them to deal with complexity, diversity, and change" (Association of American Colleges and Universities, 2013). In addition to broad knowledge, in-depth study in a discipline, and development of intellectual and practical skills, liberal education emphasizes the development of social responsibility. Multicultural initiatives—those programs and strategies that "promote skill development to better manage difference on a personal, institutional, community, or societal level" (Watt, Chapter 1 of this volume, p. 7)—support the mission of liberal education in multiple ways. One includes preparing students to be socially responsible participants in a global community. Another includes fostering skill development for managing difference within institutional contexts, such that the learning environment supports all students. Determining the success of these initiatives requires assessment, defined here as systematic examination of how well institutions achieve articulated educational intentions (Maki, 2004).

If institutions of higher education seek to promote diversity as a social value, they must help students critically explore concepts of identity, privilege, power, and systems of oppression (Watt, 2011). Multicultural initiatives have the capacity to facilitate individual and institutional change (Watt, Chapter 1 of this volume). Assessment is necessary to determine the extent to which these initiatives effectively yield intended outcomes.

This chapter outlines the foundational principle of assessment, calls on practitioners to take a broad view of the assessment of multicultural initiatives, and provides a case study of multicultural efforts at a private, residential, liberal arts college. The chapter concludes with practical suggestions for assessment of multicultural initiatives.

Assessment

Assessment has emerged as an essential element of student affairs practice (Bresciani, Moore Gardner, and Hickmott, 2009; Schuh and Upcraft, 2001). It provides a systematic means to determine the extent to which we have achieved our educational intentions (Maki, 2004). Suskie (2009) detailed assessment as an "ongoing process" involving four steps: (1) "establishing clear, measurable expected outcomes of student learning"; (2) "ensuring that students have sufficient opportunities to achieve those outcomes"; (3) "systematically gathering, analyzing, and interpreting evidence to determine how well student learning matches our expectations"; and (4) "using the resulting information to understand and improve student learning" (p. 4).

Information gleaned from assessment provides means to counter prevailing campus assumptions. For instance, with a few years of improved recruitment of students of color, arguments such as "our diversity numbers are increasing, so our campus must be welcoming and supportive" might emerge. In other cases, arguments might be made that we live in a "post-racial" and "post-gendered" society. These assertions imply that multicultural initiatives are no longer necessary. Assessment data—about student retention, community attitudes and behaviors, and campus climate, for example—can help practitioners effectively respond to these types of statements and make the case for educational practices (Schuh and Upcraft, 2001). Furthermore, assessment strategies that examine the extent to which students learn and institutional environments change as a result of multicultural initiatives help us continue to refine and improve those practices (Pope, Reynolds, and Mueller, 2004).

Case Study

The stories that opened this chapter resulted in several multicultural campus initiatives. The institution, its context, the initiatives, and the efforts to assess them are detailed in the following case study.

Cornell College.   Located in Mount Vernon, Iowa, Cornell College was founded in 1853 by a Methodist minister. Today, the College maintains an affiliation with the United Methodist Church but welcomes people from all religious traditions and nonreligious perspectives. A private, residential undergraduate liberal arts college, Cornell enrolls approximately 1,200 students (Cornell College, 2013).

Cornell College admitted white women with its first class, graduating its first female in 1858. The College's first African American graduate earned his degree in 1900. It was not until 1967 that the College graduated its first African American woman. The College's documents are decidedly quiet on the "firsts" of other students of color. Today, Cornell College's enrollment is more racially diverse, with the entering class of 2012 including 24 percent self-identified students of color and 6 percent international students.

Created in the late 1960s through student protests, the ICL provides general programs and services for all Cornell students as well as those designed specifically to meet the needs of students of color and international students. Historically, the office has been challenged with lack of guidance, no formal authority, and limited financial resources. As a result, the office served its purpose as a safe haven for African American students and other students of color, but did so without meaningful connection to the College as a whole, leading to a ghettoized existence on the periphery of campus physically and symbolically. Today, the ICL is dedicated to encouraging and implementing a more racially and culturally diverse student, faculty, and staff population while enriching the curricular and co-curricular experience for all students. The ultimate goal is to prepare students to be visionary leaders with the knowledge to effectively address the challenges of life in an intercultural world. Doing so requires multiple efforts, including (1) enhancing the campus experience for students of color and international students and (2) challenging all staff and faculty to engage in difficult dialogues about privilege and dynamics of oppression.

Cornell College Multicultural Initiatives.   Since the occurrence of the events that opened this chapter, Cornell College has undertaken a number of efforts to address social justice issues. Two multicultural initiatives taking place at the College today are "Each One Teach One," an orientation for students of color, and the Division of Student Affairs' (DSA) "Inclusion Conversations." Each is described here.

Each One Teach One.   Noting that students of color were not participating in such educational opportunities as study abroad, internships, or student-faculty research, ICL staff spoke with students and concluded that students did not participate in programs outside the ICL because they did not feel connected to the College. The ICL encouraged the College to add programs for international students and students of color to its existing new student orientation, asserting that orientation programs designed to meet their particular needs could help better connect them with all dimensions of the College. Several years later, an external review of the College's first-year programs drew similar conclusions about the experiences of students of color and international students, resulting in financial support being granted to create an additional four-day orientation program specifically for domestic students of color.

The goal of "Each One Teach One" is to introduce new students of color to Cornell College in a way that meets specific needs not addressed in New Student Orientation. For instance, the program promotes the importance of leadership development, highlights opportunities, and connects incoming students with student leaders of color. The program also creates a safe space in which students can talk openly about the culture shock experienced coming to a rural community and attending a predominantly white institution. Finally, the program seeks to enhance student connection to the institution and, as a result, improve retention.

On its surface, this program represents diversity as a social good (Watt, 2011). A multicultural initiative that promotes diversity as a social good operates within the existing context, without attempting to dismantle the systems of privilege and oppression. Each One Teach One certainly can be perceived as a "social good" in that it strives to create a space for marginalized groups of students. Certainly, the program seeks to meet these goals. However, Each One Teach One's larger goal represents diversity as a social value (Watt, 2011). Retaining larger numbers of students of color and international students and simultaneously connecting them with leadership opportunities and experiences across campus begins to alter the makeup of the student body and to challenge systems of privilege. While not sufficient, the program is a necessary step toward diversity as a social value.

Inclusion Conversations.   Similar to other colleges, the student affairs division at Cornell College began to focus increased attention on professional development specific to multicultural competence. In 2009, the staff began having monthly Inclusion Conversations, using the social justice lens and incorporating work individuals must do to understand their own identities as well as the manifestations of privilege, power, and agency in their daily interactions. Staff members come together each month in dialogue, focusing on one identity. Participating staff engage in an ongoing self-assessment of their comfort levels with the topic, discussing how it has permeated their lives throughout the past month and affected their interactions with students, faculty, and other staff.

The Inclusion Conversations allow staff to engage in authentic dialogue with one another and help foster social justice as they apply their learning in broader campus contexts. It is in these conversations that programming ideas may come forward, but more importantly, for staff members who share the commitment to engage in multicultural initiatives across campus, these conversations provide a network of colleagues who can support change and honestly discuss and assess the improvements that are possible.

This program reflects diversity as a social value (Watt, 2011). These conversations, through the sharing of individual experiences, call attention to the systems of privilege and oppression that are at play in the campus context and, in some instances, provide strategies for disrupting those systems. Although individual growth and development are program goals, the overarching intention is to change the environmental context and culture of the institution.

Assessing Cornell College Multicultural Initiatives.   Without assessment, questions about the impact or effectiveness of these multicultural initiatives would remain (Garcia and others, 2001). Cornell's assessment program is shaped by two questions adapted from Maki (2004): "How well are we achieving our educational intentions?" and "How do we know?" Efforts to assess these two initiatives fold into the overall assessment plan of the College and, thus, are guided by the same questions.

Qualitative methods provide the most robust means for answering our questions about the impact of these multicultural initiatives. First, qualitative methods closely align with the intended outcomes of both programs (Bresciani, Zelna, and Anderson, 2004). Second, qualitative assessments detail the contexts in which these programs exist, providing comprehensive, in-depth information about the institutional environment (Harper and Museus, 2007; Merriam, 1998; O'Neil Green, 2007). Third, qualitative inquiry can bring to light voices not routinely considered, particularly in terms of how students make meaning of their experiences, and, as a result, can yield multiple perspectives (Harper and Museus, 2007; O'Neil Green, 2007). Finally, assessing programs in their natural settings—with naturally occurring methods—provides holistic, complex pictures that can reveal areas for improvement (Bresciani, Moore Gardner, and Hickmott, 2009; O'Neil Green, 2007).

The use of a qualitative approach is further suggested by the overuse of surveys (Yousey-Elsener, 2011, personal communication), the limited information surveys provide (O'Neil Green, 2007), and the limitations of small sample sizes, a persistent challenge on small campuses. In the sections that follow, we describe how observations, informal interviews, and triangulation are used to assess Each One Teach One and Inclusion Conversations.

Observations.   Often underused in assessment, observations result from fieldwork and provide thick, rich descriptions of behaviors, personal interactions, group processes, and contexts (Bresciani, Moore Gardner, and Hickmott, 2009). Data can be collected through "participant observation," in which the researcher takes part in the activities associated with the phenomena being studied, or through "nonparticipant observation," wherein the researcher remains uninvolved in such activities and processes (Creswell, 2003).

Assessment of the Inclusion Conversations relies heavily on participant observation to examine program impact and effectiveness. Observation takes place both within the context of the conversation setting and the overall campus community. Because the conversations entail intensive self-reflection and openness, facilitators are able to note, within the dialogue setting itself, challenging topics of discussion, places of resistance (Watt, Chapter 1 of this volume), personal and participant change, and the effectiveness of dialogue strategies. These observations are noted after the dialogue session concludes. Facilitators and participants alike use the social justice strategy of "panning" (Obear, 2013), which means to observe the larger campus context, both in terms of campus climate and organizational change. These observations are central to the dialogues as participants note and discuss demonstrated change or examples of social injustices and microaggressions. More formally, the data yielded from these observations are discussed among the facilitators and the student affairs senior staff to identify (1) the effectiveness of dialogue strategies, (2) aggregate changes in participants' social justice knowledge and self-awareness, (3) changes in campus climate and organizational processes, and (4) areas for continued work. Results provide direction and are used for improvement of the program. These improvements include determining future topics to be covered, increasing willingness to push one another toward deeper levels of understanding, and sitting in the discomfort without finding answers. Following further bias-related incidents on campus, assessment revealed that the conversations provide a format for discussing the incident, exploring personal reactions, and processing institutional responses.

Informal Interviews. Commonly used in qualitative data collection, interviews allow researchers the opportunity to explore with individuals, or small clusters of individuals, questions about their experiences, knowledge, feelings, beliefs, and perceptions (Patton, 2002). Semi-structured interviews incorporate broad, open-ended questions scripted in advance combined with unscripted follow-up questions (Merriam, 1998).

Each One Teach One employs an informal interviewing strategy to identify effects and effectiveness of the program. It should be noted that "informal" is not synonymous with "unplanned." The focus group discussion is planned but occurs in a natural setting with an open, unstructured format. Students who participated in "Each One Teach One" are invited to a reunion event. Participants share their experiences, what they gained from the orientation, and how it has impacted their transition. The discussion, which is recorded, moves in an open, unstructured format. After the event, the staff takes notes on the students' stories, analyzes the data gleaned, and uses categorization techniques (Rossman and Rallis, 1998). They use the results to inform future Each One Teach One sessions. Feedback we received from participants led us to add a session on financial literacy with a specific focus on credit cards. We used concepts from Thomas Shapiro's (2004) book, *The Hidden Costs of Being African American*, to have in-depth conversations about inherited and intergenerational wealth to further highlight inequalities as related to students of color. We added walking tours of Mount Vernon as students cited safety as a concern and wanted to become more familiar with the community in addition to the campus. We also added a historical tour of campus that noted the contributions of people of color in order to provide a greater sense of pride in, and connection to, the institution.

Triangulation. Though not a method of data collection per se, triangulation provides a means for addressing questions of believability of assessment results, particularly those using qualitative methods (Harper, 2007; Merriam, 1998). Triangulation entails using multiple researchers, multiple methods of data collection, and multiple sources to confirm findings. With both Each One Teach One and Inclusion Conversations, overall assessment results stem from multiple strategies for gathering and analyzing data. Relevant quantitative data are used to confirm or refute findings. For instance, quantitative data provide evidence of improving retention rates, benchmarks for student engagement, and reporting of bias-related incidents.

Additional Recommendations

Paul Wellstone (2002) once said, "Never separate the life you live from the words you speak" (book jacket). One cannot merely assess the different aspects of multicultural initiatives without also becoming a change agent. Assessment of multicultural initiatives is best conducted alongside an intentional understanding of the ways in which researchers bring their own bias, or often in this area, privilege, to the conversation. Good assessment must begin with self-reflection, highlighting privilege, bias, and oppression.

In addition, to foster an atmosphere of feedback, one must consider how assessment information might be used and incorporate it into daily practice. Some suggestions include the following:

- Include students. Go beyond quick post-event evaluations to consider how student experiences might be shaped by knowing they have a voice in the process.
- Talk with colleagues. To better understand what is happening in arenas across campus, explore these questions with colleagues. Perhaps someone has heard feedback that has implications for your program in another department. Create open avenues for communicating.
- Explore the student experience as a whole rather than the experiences of one. Examining the individual experience is important to meet individual student needs, but for assessment, the whole—the aggregate student experience—is most important.
- Analyze data gleaned from focus groups and interviews to determine whether student experiences are transferable (Merriam, 1998) to the broader campus context.

Similar to multicultural initiatives, assessment must become a part of the fabric of campus. Increased comfort with methods—formal and informal, quantitative and qualitative—allows us to create environments where students share experiences through stories and the examination of observable outcomes becomes a routine element of departmental practice. The information gathered through these efforts, when applied, affords us opportunities to strengthen our multicultural initiatives to have greater effects on our students and campuses.

New Directions for Student Services • DOI: 10.1002/ss

References

Association of American Colleges and Universities (AAC&U). *What Is a 21st Century Liberal Education?* Retrieved January 13, 2013, from http://www.aacu.org/leap/what_is_liberal_education.cfm

Bresciani, M. J., Moore Gardner, M., and Hickmott, J. *Demonstrating Student Success: A Practical Guide to Outcomes-Based Assessment.* Sterling, Va.: Stylus Publishing, 2009.

Bresciani, M. J., Zelna, C. L., and Anderson, J. A. *Assessing Student Learning and Development: A Handbook for Practitioners.* Washington, D.C.: National Association of Student Personnel Administrators, 2004.

Cornell College. *History and Traditions.* Retrieved January 13, 2013, from http://www.cornellcollege.edu/about-cornell/history-and-traditions/index.shtml

Creswell, J. W. *Research Design: Qualitative, Quantitative, and Mixed Methods Approaches.* 2nd ed. Thousand Oaks, Calif.: Sage, 2003.

Elkins, B. "Report on Student Success by Race." *Institutional Research and Assessment.* Mount Vernon, Iowa: Cornell College, 2008.

Garcia, M., Hudgins, C. A., Musil, C. M., Nettles, M. T., Sedlacek, W. E., and Smith, D. G. *Assessing Campus Diversity Initiatives: A Guide for Campus Practitioners.* Washington, D.C.: Association of American Colleges and Universities, 2001.

Harper, S. "Using Qualitative Methods to Assess Student Trajectories and College Impact." In S. Harper and S. Museus (eds.), *Using Qualitative Methods in Institutional Assessment.* New Directions for Institutional Research, no. 136, 55–68. San Francisco: Jossey-Bass, 2007.

Harper, S., and Museus, S. (eds.). *Using Qualitative Methods in Institutional Assessment.* New Directions for Institutional Research, no. 136. San Francisco: Jossey-Bass, 2007.

Maki, P. L. *Assessing for Learning: Building a Sustainable Commitment Across the Institution.* Sterling, Va.: Stylus Publishing, 2004.

Merriam, S. B. *Qualitative Research and Case Study Applications in Education.* San Francisco: Jossey-Bass, 1998.

Obear, K. *Infusing Diversity into Everything We Do.* Retrieved January 13, 2013, from http://drkathyobear.com/article-blog/

O'Neil Green, D. "Using Qualitative Methods to Assess Academic Success and Retention Programs for Underrepresented Minority Students." In S. Harper and S. Museus (eds.), *Using Qualitative Methods in Institutional Assessment.* New Directions for Institutional Research, no. 136, 41–53. San Francisco: Jossey-Bass, 2007.

Patton, M. Q. *Qualitative Research and Evaluation Methods.* Thousand Oaks, Calif.: Sage, 2002.

Pope, R. L., Reynolds, A. L., and Mueller, J. A. *Multicultural Competence in Student Affairs.* San Francisco: Jossey-Bass, 2004.

Rossman, G. B., and Rallis, S. F. *Learning in the Field: An Introduction to Qualitative Research.* Thousand Oaks, Calif.: Sage, 1998.

Schuh, J. H., and Upcraft, M. L. *Assessment Practice in Student Affairs: An Applications Manual.* San Francisco: Jossey-Bass, 2001.

Shapiro, T. *The Hidden Costs of Being African American: How Wealth Perpetuates Inequality.* New York: Oxford University Press, 2004.

Suskie, L. *Assessing Student Learning: A Common Sense Guide.* 2nd ed. San Francisco: Jossey-Bass, 2009.

Watt, S. K. "Moving Beyond the Talk: From Difficult Dialogues to Action." In J. Arminio, V. Torres, and R. Pope (eds.), *Why Aren't We There Yet: Taking Personal*

Responsibility for Creating an Inclusive Campus. Sterling, Va.: Stylus Publishing, 2011.

Wellstone, P. *The Conscience of a Liberal: Reclaiming the Compassionate Agenda.* Minneapolis: University of Minnesota Press, 2002.

BECKI ELKINS *is the registrar and director of institutional research and assessment at Cornell College.*

KENNETH MORRIS, JR., *is the director of intercultural life at Cornell College.*

GWENDOLYN SCHIMEK *is the assistant dean of students and director of student life at Cornell College and a doctoral student in college and university leadership at Colorado State University.*

NEW DIRECTIONS FOR STUDENT SERVICES • DOI: 10.1002/ss

3

This chapter summarizes the implementation of a campus-wide multicultural initiative at a large public Midwestern university, exploring strategies, challenges, and lessons learned.

Building and Sustaining a Campus-Wide Multicultural Initiative

Georgina Dodge, Lindsay Jarratt

The challenge of developing effective multicultural training for all facets of a complex university organization is a daunting task. The desire to foster diverse and inclusive campus environments often results in "one-size-fits-all" programs or a buffet of different workshops focused on various identities or affinity groups. These approaches are problematic because they typically do not include multiple and intersecting dimensions of identity and ignore the need for nuanced approaches to examining intrapersonal, interpersonal, and societal and systemic dimensions of diversity, inclusion, and equity (Bell and Griffin, 2007). Instituting and sustaining multicultural initiatives at a predominantly white institution can also be challenging because those initiatives are rooted in programs that either become the exclusive property of already marginalized groups or are seen as oppressive tools in the hands of the majority (McHatton, Keller, Shircliffe, and Zalaquett, 2009; Wildman, 1996).

The Context

The University of Iowa is representative of predominantly white large public institutions undergoing change. While demographics at the university are shifting, a long history of low numbers of racial minorities has led to a culture of homogenization where "colorblind" attitudes are adopted and race, in addition to all forms of difference, is leveled by community-valued attributes such as work ethic. But the influx of students, staff, and faculty from around the world has resulted in the presence of diverse viewpoints and experiences that require creating an environment in which all identities are respected and treated equitably.

When Dodge arrived on campus as the Chief Diversity Officer three years ago, there was demand for some type of diversity training with clear, consistent messaging and far-reaching impact. Though many pockets of

New Directions for Student Services, no. 144, Winter 2013 © 2013 Wiley Periodicals, Inc.
Published online in Wiley Online Library (wileyonlinelibrary.com) • DOI: 10.1002/ss.20066

inclusion efforts had formed to address this need, much of the work was siloed and reaching limited populations. Additionally, a small but passionate group of advocates and allies were carrying a very large responsibility in trying to create safe spaces, foster dialogue, teach and raise awareness, create skill-development opportunities, and advocate for changes in policy or practice, in addition to their regular workloads.

The Model: National Coalition Building Institute

In order to meet the diverse and ever-changing needs of our campus, we turned to the National Coalition Building Institute (NCBI), a model with which both authors had prior experience. Our interest in the model was driven not by the intent to make it *the* diversity training for the campus but to establish a nucleus around which other programming could develop and to provide support for individuals and groups working to further the university's goals for diversity and inclusion. We see NCBI as supplying tools for individuals who promote social change, in keeping with the "diversity as a value versus good" philosophy that Watt (2007, Chapter 1 of this volume) espouses in the introductory chapter of this volume. Diversity as a value philosophy occurs in part due to the NCBI model's focus on inter- and intra-cultural relationship development and not just a primary focus on targeting and oppression.

Using approaches that align with the multicultural social justice education framework (Sleeter and Grant, 2007), NCBI is dedicated to the elimination of all forms of oppression (National Coalition Building Institute, 2003). Both authors had been through NCBI's facilitator training and appreciated the manner in which NCBI relies on interaction among all identities, providing space for considering how past experiences have shaped our knowledge and understanding, and engaging in healing work while enabling participants to develop knowledge, skills, and awareness that contribute to the initiative's growth and sustainability.

NCBI has 31 "affiliates" on campuses in the United States (as well as teams in corporations, K–12 schools, and communities around the world) that consist of teams trained by NCBI to provide proactive responses to discrimination and intergroup conflict. NCBI has won numerous awards and been lauded for its international diversity training work, and there is a notable lack of published critique but a simultaneous need for further research into the impact and effectiveness of NCBI's campus models.

Gaining Institutional Support

While we continue to develop our own evidence of the initiative's efficacy, we are not prevented from recognizing the "fit" between NCBI and a predominantly white institution: NCBI provides space to explore white identity (and other dominant identities) alongside and in relation to the multitude

NEW DIRECTIONS FOR STUDENT SERVICES • DOI: 10.1002/ss

of marginalized identities that are usually the focus of multicultural teachings. From a philosophical perspective, this inclusive focus acknowledges and honors the richness of each person's interconnected identities, as well as inviting deeper interrogation into the ways in which our identities and experiences are shaped within larger societal structures. However, the issue of fit with the institutional culture is important not only for the relevance of programming but also for the ability to gain buy-in from decision makers and administrative sponsors who need to see the initiative as a worthwhile investment of staff time as well as the institution's funds. From an administrative perspective, NCBI's inclusion of all identities helps to alleviate the need to develop and send staff to multiple workshops focused on individual identity groups. (Although we must note here that we are not advocating for a cessation of such workshops.)

Admittedly, implementation of such a comprehensive model does require a commitment of significant financial resources. Though the cost of affiliation with the national organization is relatively minimal, costs to bring NCBI leaders to campus for an exposure workshop and to train campus members through a "Train-the-Trainer" incur an initial price tag that may deter some campuses. However, once start-up costs have been covered, the initiative becomes largely self-sustaining. Additionally, the benefits of being connected to experienced ongoing support and resources, as well as being able to focus energy on implementation rather than a lengthy content-development process, add to the value of our relationship with NCBI. It is difficult to compare what our potential costs might have been had we chosen to develop a similarly structured model ourselves; however, it is certain that the amount of time involved in developing a meaningful and tangible initiative would have been substantial.

Weaving an initiative of any type into the campus fabric requires clear direction supported by strong organization. The effort inevitably faces logistical challenges inherent in any attempt to provide consistent and broad-reaching messages within the complex and diverse web of often highly autonomous departments and campus units. Recognizing this, Dodge gave the initiative a central home within the Chief Diversity Office, built leadership of the initiative and campus affiliate into position descriptions, and hired Jarratt as the director of the initiative to provide a single point of contact for campus and to direct ongoing development. Jarratt's position is supported by an assistant director for increased effectiveness and decreased isolation for her role. While Jarratt holds other responsibilities, a significant amount of her time and effort are dedicated to NCBI, an investment on behalf of the unit and the university in the initiative. This investment has already paid off simply through the accessibility of diversity and equity training to the campus community, but it will not be possible to measure overall impact on campus climate for some time, as we are still in our second year.

The NCBI model's focus on a coalition-building approach requires significant buy-in from campus constituencies, particularly the commitment of the individual faculty and staff as well as the department's investment of time to attend workshops and/or to become involved with ongoing affiliate work. For some departments or positions, subtle embedded structures of elitism and institutionalized oppression within the academy create disparities in individuals' abilities to participate. While some staff members—particularly administrative and support staff—report difficulties in obtaining release time to participate in ways that feel meaningful, we hear from faculty—particularly women and faculty of color—that the disproportionate expectations of service placed on their shoulders make it more difficult to participate, even if they have a strong interest.

While navigating some of these larger structural and institutional constraints will undoubtedly be an evolving process, we have worked to ensure that senior campus leadership is aware of our effort and familiar with the initiative. During an annual retreat, the President's Cabinet participated in an abridged workshop that exposed them to the key principles and strategies of the initiative, assessment data so far, and ongoing conversation about future potential for NCBI and the campus affiliate to support achievement of the university's strategic goals. We also continue to invite senior leaders to champion our efforts by inviting them to attend or speak at events or programs, as well as providing them with current assessment data so that they can speak comfortably and knowledgeably about our work and how it benefits the campus community. Of course, not all of our leaders have transitioned from recognizing the initiative as a social value rather than merely a social good (Watt, 2011, Chapter 1 of this volume), but the continuous nature of the initiative enables us to nurture that development as we move forward.

The Participant Experience

Integrating NCBI into the campus fabric is a multifaceted process, as the intent is not to provide a single experience, or even a series of experiences, that somehow provides all the tools and awareness necessary for individuals to be effective advocates for equity and inclusion. While training and workshop models that prompt reflection, awareness, and skill development are integral to the initiative, the larger intent is to create a resource for campus thinking and engagement rooted in a foundation of coalition. In other words, we seek to create a campus initiative, as defined by Watt in the introductory chapter, rather than a singular program. Nonetheless, most individuals who become aware of the campus NCBI initiative do so through participation in one of the workshops developed by NCBI and offered on campus by affiliate members. The workshops' significance as primary access points into deeper connection with the NCBI initiative makes it essential to maintain attentiveness to oversight of workshops, facilitators, and participant experiences.

New Directions for Student Services • DOI: 10.1002/ss

NCBI has developed several workshop and training models, two of which have been integrated as part of our campus initiative. The primary workshop, which we title "Leadership for Equity and Inclusion," is a day-long experience where participants are prompted to engage in self-reflection and interpersonal dialogue as the group explores information and misinformation we have learned about our own identities and others', shares personal stories of the impacts of oppression, and gains skills for recognizing and responding to hurtful interactions. More recently, we have also integrated a half-day workshop, "Controversial Issues," in which participants, using a real experience of controversy, gain skills to lead constructively through tough conflicts in ways that enable disputing parties to move toward future cooperation. In both workshops, participants are engaged in reflection, activities, and dialogue that use social and emotional learning to connect with intellectual concepts (Elias, 2003) to help them gain awareness and skills that will lead to confidence and efficacy in efforts to nurture authentic inclusion and equity.

The highly personal and emotional nature of the learning environment created in the workshops makes it inevitable that many participants will experience dissonance or resistance (Watt, 2007). Within a workshop experience, it may not be possible—or even desirable—to resolve participant dissonance but there is intentional space created and attention directed to recognizing our personal responses to material, and participants are encouraged to embrace moments of dissonance rather than avoiding, disputing, or discounting them. Perhaps for this reason, resistant dynamics have not manifested as often as we anticipated considering the topic, approach, and our demographic population as a predominantly white institution. In fact, workshop attendees often express pleasant surprise at the unexpected diversity on campus and gain a better understanding of others' perspectives, whether those positions are related to personal identity or affiliation, disciplinary culture, or other factors.

Our information about participant response comes largely from a pre- and post-assessment completed by participants (discussed in more detail later), so at this stage we are somewhat speculative as to why we are seeing less resistance than we expected. Perhaps we have not yet struck the most effective balance of challenge and support necessary to create an experience that helps participants acknowledge, confront, and begin to unlearn "knowledge" of the world that is actually rooted in misinformation that enables us to justify a noninclusive, nonequitable status quo. But we also must explore the possibility that specific strategies developed by NCBI and implemented by our team (such as team facilitation with wide representation of identities) may be effective at lowering defenses and encouraging people to "sit with discomfort" (Watt, 2007, p. 115) without disengaging. We have identified this as a critical area for the focus of future research and discussion.

Ongoing Facilitator and Team Development

At the core of each workshop is the affiliate coalition, which makes this initiative unique and increases its potential for effecting cultural paradigm shifts on campus in a sustained way. The affiliate consists of students, staff, and faculty who, after completing the one-day workshop, continue by attending a three-day train-the-trainer. This skill development is ongoing as our affiliate meets regularly to practice, discuss relevant issues, and participate together in other training opportunities. The development of deeper trust and dialogue across identities represented in our team of 50 affiliate members is a model for the work we attempt to do in workshops and our strategic change efforts. And the impact of individual affiliate members on their home departments provides opportunity for those outside the affiliate to witness inclusive behavior and to begin understanding how differences can coexist within departmental environments.

The very existence of the team also helps ensure sustainability of the program. As those invested in equity work can attest, leadership of diversity and inclusion efforts can be fairly isolating and exhausting, but within this model, no one leads alone. Workshops are facilitated by teams, and even leadership of the affiliate is structured to minimize isolation. And when we encounter resistance from workshop participants—or even from among the affiliate—the established trust and alliance provides a foundation for working through issues. Working with the affiliate also provides one way that we can be transparent in our interactions on campus, inviting broad participation in inclusion efforts. For this reason, ongoing development for affiliate members and the team is central to our strategy as we seek to build a team that is widely representative of our campus community. In the future, we hope to employ our affiliate as a brain trust to help develop other programming, such as an outreach group to assist with handling informal complaints of bias on campus. Taken in this light, the initial investment in building the team has the potential to yield exponential results within our greater community.

Campus Perceptions and Response

Partly due to the complex nature of a large university, response from the broader campus community is difficult to pinpoint concretely and information must be inferred from rates of participation and requests from departments who are seeking involvement with the initiative or, conversely, from barriers or challenges to the initiative. We have seen an increase in levels of individual participation since NCBI's inception on our campus two years ago: our initial workshops often had 10–15 participants; now, our numbers are generally closer to 25–30. In total, over seven hundred faculty, staff, and students from our campus have attended a workshop led by NCBI members.

NEW DIRECTIONS FOR STUDENT SERVICES • DOI: 10.1002/ss

Additionally, there are pockets of the campus community that have begun to explore ways in which we can partner for greater impact, and we have received requests to adapt workshops to meet specific needs within units. We are focusing energy in these places of natural coalition.

We have also begun to notice a new pattern that seems indicative of campus acceptance, although this pattern is a double-edged sword. As our participation grows, more participants are sharing that they were mandated or strongly urged to attend by supervisors. This can lead to increased resistance in workshops, but it may also indicate that those in positions of authority see NCBI as a resource with positive impact for their workforce.

That is not to say that the campus response has been wholly supportive. From some individuals involved in other multicultural and inclusion efforts on campus there has been a high level of scrutiny of the model and its implementation. Our information on this issue is more anecdotal in nature, but critiques of the initiative fall into one of two categories: (1) questions regarding the philosophical framework and its effectiveness or appropriateness, particularly rooted in a discomfort with the emotional nature of content; and (2) concerns regarding allocation of resources, particularly financial, and perceptions of competition that lead to questions of value or perceived value. To the first concern, we acknowledge the benefit—and indeed the need—for multiple approaches to inclusion efforts, but we hold firm to the necessity of emotional connection in multicultural education (Watt, 2007). As to the second set of concerns, it is important that our team demonstrates in the long term that the presence of an NCBI affiliate engaged in coalition building with critical consciousness is and will continue to be worth the investment.

Assessing Impact

Our current formal method of evaluation consists of an anonymous pre- and post-workshop assessment adapted from a tool developed by NCBI that examines relevant participant beliefs before and after the workshop, learning outcomes, and satisfaction with the workshop. While we intend a more in-depth analysis of data collected to present in the future, we are pleased that built into the workshop experience are spaces that provide significant measures of impact for participants' expressions of self-pride, trust in and comfort with others, understanding of the impact of oppression and discrimination, and willingness and confidence to attempt addressing wrongs or making change.

The open-ended commentary collected has been overwhelmingly positive and includes statements such as "For the first time, I don't feel alone. You made Iowa feel more like home," and "This was, without a doubt, the best experience I have had in the last 15 years of working at the University of Iowa." Of course, there have been criticisms as well, focusing primarily on individual discomfort with the often emotional nature of the workshop.

But what we find most remarkable is that from all evaluations collected, only 2 percent include any level of critical feedback. And when asked if they would recommend the experience to colleagues, 99 percent of respondents indicate that they would. We are learning from all feedback as we tailor the model, and we continue to look for deeper and broader ways to assess campus impact.

The Journey Continues

Even as we continue to develop evaluation metrics, we received an exhilarating yet intimidating endorsement from NCBI National when we were asked to host the NCBI 20th Annual Campus Conference in November 2012. Campus affiliate members from across the country and Canada attended the event, and we were proud to showcase our affiliate, campus, and hometown. Both our president and provost attended the opening reception and welcomed attendees with remarks that emphasized the university's commitment to inclusion and the importance of diversity on our campus. They visibly demonstrated their support of our efforts and their remarks connected our work to the advancement of campus strategic goals, a message that resonated not only with guests to our campus but with those on campus who had invested significantly in the initiative and in the development of the conference.

A group of participants from our sister institution, the University of Northern Iowa, attended the conference, which gave us an opportunity to develop closer connections with that affiliate. We are now discussing the possibility of forming a statewide coalition to support each other's efforts. The conference also enabled us to strengthen our connection to NCBI International. While we currently have informational and supportive phone meetings with our NCBI campus liaison, it was energizing to learn from the wisdom of long-time trainers and activists who have dedicated their working lives to diversity and inclusion. We heard the history of the organization from those who made that history, and we absorbed lessons to guide us moving forward.

We continue strategizing for the challenges ahead. Our greatest concern is the ongoing need for resources to sustain the overall model. While the financial support has become less significant, the demand for time and talent of facilitators increases. Competent facilitators are crucial for the model's bedrock, but we also recognize that it is difficult for facilitators to invest a full day away from routine duties and we have developed shorter exercises to meet the diverse needs of campus units.

In our opinion, the initiative serves not only to create a welcoming campus climate but also to help prepare our students—and ourselves—for a world under continuous change. Change = difference = diversity, and the tools we develop for living in diverse environments enable us to thrive. As our inclusion efforts expand, our ability to help campus leaders become social change agents—and vice versa—is a primary goal. Our campus initiative is merely the start of a values shift that we hope will change the very nature of campus. We gain encouragement from knowing that our work benefits our future.

References

Bell, L., and Griffin, P. "Designing Social Justice Education Courses." In M. Adams, L. A. Bell, and P. Griffin (eds.), *Teaching for Diversity and Social Justice*. New York: Routledge, 2007.

Elias, M. J. *Academic and Social-Emotional Learning*, 2003. Retrieved February 20, 2013, from http://www.ibe.unesco.org/fileadmin/user_upload/archive/publications/EducationalPracticesSeriesPdf/prac11e.pdf

McHatton, P. A., Keller, H., Shircliffe, B., and Zalaquett, C. "Examining Efforts to Infuse Diversity Within One College of Education." *Journal of Diversity in Higher Education*, 2009, 2(3), 127–135.

National Coalition Building Institute. *Principles into Practice: Strengthening Leadership for a Diverse Society*. Washington, D.C.: National Coalition Building Institute, 2003.

Sleeter, C. E., and Grant, C. A. *Making Choices for Multicultural Education: Five Approaches to Race, Class, and Gender*. 5th ed. Hoboken, N.J.: John Wiley & Sons, Inc., 2007.

Watt, S. "Difficult Dialogues, Privilege and Social Justice: Uses of the Privileged Identity Exploration (PIE) Model in Student Affairs Practice." *The College Student Affairs Journal*, 2007, 26(2), 114–125.

Watt, S. K. "Moving Beyond the Talk: From Difficult Dialogues to Action." In J. Arminio, V. Torres, and R. Pope (eds.), *Why Aren't We There Yet: Taking Personal Responsibility for Creating an Inclusive Campus*. Sterling, Va.: Stylus Publishing, 2011.

Wildman, S. *How Invisible Preference Undermines America*. New York: New York University Press, 1996.

GEORGINA DODGE *is the chief diversity officer and associate vice president at the University of Iowa and an adjunct associate professor of English. She is also an experienced diversity trainer.*

LINDSAY JARRATT *is a diversity resources coordinator at the University of Iowa and directs the Campus Affiliate of the National Coalition Building Institute. She is also an experienced diversity trainer.*

NEW DIRECTIONS FOR STUDENT SERVICES • DOI: 10.1002/ss

4

This chapter explores the design and implementation of service learning as a multicultural initiative. The author shares considerations for multicultural service-learning practice using an example from a course project focused on leadership skill development in public service.

Navigating Difference through Multicultural Service Learning

Kira Pasquesi

I am here to challenge you to recognize your inability, your powerlessness and your incapacity to do the "good" which you intended to do. I am here to entreat you to use your money, your status and your education to travel in Latin America. Come to look, come to climb our mountains, to enjoy our flowers. Come to study. But do not come to help.

(Illich, 2012, p. 81)

This excerpt from Ivan Illich's famous 1968 address "To Hell with Good Intentions" was delivered for American volunteers serving in Mexico. Illich challenged the paternalistic nature of international service missions that situates "haves" in service to "have nots." Like other service-learning practitioners in higher education, I used Illich's remarks to discuss the unintended consequences of service with college students. While service has the potential to foster new insights about social problems and deeper understandings across difference, it can also reinforce stereotypes and sustain systems of inequality.

As a white, female, heterosexual, and middle class practitioner at a small liberal arts college, I facilitated service-learning experiences that combined relevant community-based projects with course content and guided reflection. In this role, I worked to challenge undergraduate students' assumptions about individuals they encountered during service-learning placements. I taught students to apply a variety of community-based methods in order to recognize the abundant yet often unacknowledged resources and strengths in local communities. I confronted the ways in which students positioned individuals at their service placements as inherently different from themselves during reflection activities and in response to journal

New Directions for Student Services, no. 144, Winter 2013 © 2013 Wiley Periodicals, Inc.
Published online in Wiley Online Library (wileyonlinelibrary.com) • DOI: 10.1002/ss.20067

entries. Looking back, I realize that these efforts, even with the best of intentions, reinforced some of the very social hierarchies and injustices I was working to disrupt. Students also walked away from their experiences without the skills necessary to critically examine the social and political context that created the need for service in the first place.

Watt (2011) refers to efforts like these, and others on college campuses, as motivated by the principle of "diversity as good" (p. 131). Practices stemming from this conceptual frame function largely within established societal structures without an attempt to analyze and disrupt underlying or system-level problems (Watt, 2011). Service learning as a "social good" can reproduce divides between members of dominant and marginalized populations in community settings. It can also limit students' capacities to develop skills to better manage difference and ultimately influence social change.

Skill development in understanding and navigating difference on a variety of levels (personal, institutional, community, and social) is the foundation of a multicultural initiative in higher education (Watt, Chapter 1 of this volume). When designed and implemented as a multicultural initiative, service learning has the potential to contribute to a culture whereby community partners, students, faculty, administrators, and staff with shared interests in community issues can engage with difference through collaborative social action. It can also foster relationships within and between groups that grapple with the inequalities and root causes necessary to create sustainable changes in policies, structures, and institutions (Boyle-Baise, 2002).

The purpose of this chapter is to explore the intentions behind service learning as a multicultural initiative and how service learning can facilitate students' skill development in managing difference. I situate the discussion of service learning as a multicultural initiative in my experiences designing and implementing a course project on leadership for social change at a large public university. During the project, undergraduate students worked in teams to analyze the positive and negative perceptions of various stakeholder groups in a highly visible and utilized campus-community space. In the first section of the chapter, I introduce service learning and multicultural service learning. I then examine the process of designing and implementing a course project as a multicultural initiative. Finally, I conclude with recommendations for student affairs practitioners and faculty members facilitating multicultural service-learning initiatives in higher education.

Service Learning and Multicultural Service Learning

Over the past twenty years, service learning as an educational philosophy and practice has become popular throughout higher education. The Campus Compact, a national organization committed to service learning in higher education, currently boasts over 1,200 institutional members (Campus Compact, 2013). With the expansion of service-learning efforts across the higher education spectrum, there is little consensus among practitioners on a definition (Mitchell, 2008a). However, many of the definitions in the literature recognize the linking of academic work with engagement in a community (Butin, 2008). Countless descriptions also acknowledge the degrees that service learning operates "within a framework of respect, reciprocity, relevance, and reflection" (Butin, 2008, p. 77). For the purpose of this chapter, I use the term service learning to define a thoughtfully planned community-based action connected to skill development, course content, and ongoing reflection.

In many ways, the practice of service learning is well suited for educating students to understand and navigate difference. Researchers have documented that service learning can enhance students' cultural awareness, leadership abilities, and communication skills (Astin, Vogelgesang, Ikeda, and Yee, 2000). Additionally, researchers have reported that when done well, service learning has a positive effect on facilitating understanding across difference and reducing stereotypes (Eyler, Giles, Stenson, and Gray, 2001). However, at the same time, critical scholars have questioned assumptions about community partnerships and representations of "the other" without an examination of privilege and power (for example, Endres and Gould, 2009; Seider and Hillman, 2011; Sperling, 2007). Approaches to service learning have also been criticized for causing more harm than good through patronizing relationships and a deficit-based approach to community service (for example, Butin, 2006; Eby, 1998; Weah, Cornelia, and Hall, 2000).

Stemming from the critiques or limits of service learning, an emerging body of educational literature advocates for an approach to service learning termed multicultural service learning (also known as critical service learning; Boyle-Baise, 2002; Butin, 2008; Cipolle, 2010; Mitchell, 2008b; O'Grady, 2000; Rhoads, 1997). Multicultural service learning reflects the integration of multicultural education with service-learning practice in an intentional effort to build community and challenge inequality (Boyle-Baise, 2002). This is in contrast to traditional notions of service learning emphasizing the development of good citizens detached from the skills necessary to manage conflict and interact across difference. Multicultural service learning can enhance understanding of causes of injustice in order for students to see themselves as social change agents (Mitchell, 2008b).

Service Learning as a Multicultural Initiative

Leadership and Public Service is a yearlong course designed for undergraduate students with an interest in developing leadership skills for public service roles. In the fall semester, students consider how their identities, power, privilege, and oppression shape their understanding of the world and position as a leader and public servant. During the spring, students apply their learning to one-on-one mentoring relationships with middle- or high-school students and a public service project examining issues of diversity in our community. For the purpose of this chapter, I will focus on my experiences facilitating the public service project as a multicultural initiative.

The Old Capitol Mall is an indoor shopping structure centrally located in the heart of a downtown in a small Midwestern city and adjacent to the large public university campus. The mall is home to a variety of local businesses (restaurants, shops, pharmacy, bank, and newspaper headquarters) as well as a variety of university departments (International Programs, School of Music, Information Technology Services). The Old Capitol Mall is also home to the downtown transportation hub for city transit services. Bus patrons gather inside and outside the building as they wait for buses to arrive, producing large crowds during peak hours. The bus system services a wide variety of users, including university faculty, staff, students, and middle- or high-school students. Many local families living in low-income neighborhoods outside of the downtown campus region depend on public transportation, and subsequently, frequent the transit hub at the mall on a daily basis. This public transportation system is also frequented not only by university students, faculty, and others without cars or those who desire the ease of transportation during inclement weather, but also by those in the community with environmentally conscious intentions to reduce the use of gas and pollutants in the air.

As a graduate student, I utilize the Old Capitol Mall and transit hub multiple times a day for various academic or personal needs. While waiting for my bus to arrive at the transit hub, I began to notice a pattern that motivated my interest in the mall as a site for critical investigation. Groups of predominantly black teenagers would congregate at the mall while waiting for their buses to arrive after school hours. Soon business owners of the adjacent storefronts began to post signs warning about the consequences of loitering. Building management increased security operations during after school hours and implemented a revised code of conduct and mall policies. I also began to take note of the ways in which white bus patrons began waiting for their buses at a distance from the groups of black middle- and high-school students. On one occasion, I was standing at the entrance of the mall and witnessed a security guard ask a black man to remove his baseball cap in order to adhere to mall policy. After seeing this interaction, I approached the security guard and asked if I also needed to remove my winter hat. He explained the mall policy was not really intended for "people like me" and I did not have to worry about it. These observations reflect just a few of the complex interactions involving multiple and diverse stakeholder groups that motivated my interest in the space as a focus for a developing multicultural initiative.

The goals for the project included that students would (1) critically analyze issues related to diversity in the Old Capitol Mall from the perspective of an assigned stakeholder group; (2) reflect on their identity and position as related to the environment of the mall (policies, administration, and physical space); and (3) practice social action skills that can be applied to future contexts. The teams were all charged with educating themselves and their peers about the issues in the environment related to race, social class, ability, and gender. This required the students to also consider how their personal identities influenced how they viewed conflicts and interactions across difference in the space. The students conducted observations, researched news stories, investigated policies and historical context of the space, and interviewed relevant stakeholders. The project culminated in presentations to stakeholders on a recommended course of action to enhance interactions across difference rooted in their analysis of the stakeholder group and personal exploration.

As a multicultural initiative, students conducted their critical analysis of the Old Capitol Mall on multiple levels, which include the personal, community, and institutional. Through observations and interviews, they examined the policies, structures, and subtle expectations that dictate behavior and interaction in the mall. They engaged in conversation with peers and stakeholders about how decisions are made in the mall, who benefits, and conscious and unconscious responses to marginalization.

Students' intellectual and personal exploration of engaging across difference provided the foundation for the multilevel investigation. Students reflected on the ways in which their personal identities influenced how they experienced the space by asking themselves three questions whenever they visited the mall: "How am I like no one else here? How am I like some others here? And how am I like everyone here?" (Komives, 1994, p. 219). In order to practice the skills necessary for understanding and navigating difference, assignments built upon one another to guide students through a process of defining their task and purpose, understanding their distinct stakeholder group in the space, and designing a plan of action.

Facilitating Multicultural Service Learning

My experiences with the Old Capitol Mall project highlight some of the choices we make as educators in designing and implementing service learning as a multicultural initiative. In the following sections, I describe some of the challenges I encountered with the Leadership and Public Service course and the implications for facilitating service learning as a multicultural initiative.

My decisions about project design and approach to cultivating relationships all had implications for the effectiveness of the project as a multicultural initiative. Donahue (2011) explains that educators navigate conflicting values in classroom and community settings that present "teaching dilemmas" (p. 17) in service learning. When considering project design, I defined the nature and type of public service for the project. In this example, the service rested in the students' critical consciousness raising and communicating recommendations to stakeholders. By examining position and negative perceptions in the mall, students worked to develop their skills of critical analysis and social action that can be applied to future contexts. I struggled, and continue to struggle, with focusing on student consciousness over creating a sustainable impact on a contentious space that has implications for diversity and inclusion in our community. However, the rationale for this decision rested in the students' preparedness to take on a shared endeavor in collaboration with a community organization without the necessary foundation of a critical understanding of the social and political context. Instead, a representative from a city task force engaged in a discussion with the students about citizen-driven and local government efforts to promote equity and inclusion in relation to transportation services. The students shared their observations of interactions at the mall, while the representative taught the students about local social action processes.

Educators can facilitate rich and meaningful opportunities for learning when they make dilemmas in service learning explicit (Donahue, 2011). Often in service-learning reflection, students are asked to reflect on others instead of how their own perspectives and backgrounds shape how they view the communities they are a part of (Rice and Pollack, 2000). In working through service-learning dilemmas with students, educators can model the type of personal self-exploration necessary as the foundation of social change work. It requires service-learning educators to commit to the same ongoing personal development and critical reflection that we ask of our students. This development occurs by uncovering our backgrounds and biases and in educating ourselves about the historical, theoretical, and pedagogical foundations of service learning and multicultural education. It means not only asking questions of ourselves but also of those around us.

Additional Considerations for Practice

Looking back at my experiences facilitating a multicultural initiative, I learned lessons that can be applied to multicultural service-learning practice.

Preparation Is Key.   We often think of the "work" in service-learning experiences as the hands-on engagement that occurs in a community-based setting. However, the example of the Leadership and Public Service course highlights the importance of the intellectual and emotional preparation necessary prior to engaging in collective social action with community partners. The multilevel critical analysis of the Old Capitol Mall facilitated enhanced understanding of the systematic ways in which an institution can advantage some members of society at the disadvantage of others. If the students were to engage in multicultural service learning without preparation, any type of action could further reproduce the very stereotypes the project was attempting to dispel in the first place.

NEW DIRECTIONS FOR STUDENT SERVICES • DOI: 10.1002/ss

The Timeframe Matters.   If I could do it over again, I would have introduced the Old Capitol Mall project to students during the fall semester. I could have complemented the students' exploration of personal identities and privileged or targeted group memberships. This would have afforded additional time in the spring semester for collective group action and continued skill development. The students would have also begun forming important relationships with members of stakeholder groups. It is important to be realistic about the timeframe for multicultural service learning and the capacity of the students to deliver sustainable initiatives alongside of community partners given scheduling constraints.

Begin with Individual Action.   Looking back, I also would have focused more intentionally throughout the Old Capitol Mall project on the ways in which students could assume roles as educators in sharing their learning with roommates, peers, and family members. This introduces students to social action early on in the process and scaffolds any future social action done in collaboration with others. Student participants in multicultural service learning can identify ways to hold each other accountable for individual action during the experience and after the completion of the course.

Ongoing Facilitator Skill Development.   In facilitating service learning as a multicultural initiative, student affairs practitioners and faculty members will be increasingly asked to work across divisions, offices, and campus-community lines. This will require collaboration with chief diversity officers, community leaders, and student affairs practitioners in offices such as multicultural student services. Practitioners and faculty members engaged in service learning will also require the skills necessary to facilitate difficult dialogues. A difficult dialogue involves an exchange of beliefs and experiences between community members that raise conflicting viewpoints about diversity (Watt, 2007). These skills will be integral in cultivating relationships with community partners and facilitating reflection to raise critical consciousness.

Closing Thoughts

This chapter highlights an application of service learning as a multicultural initiative aimed at developing skills to understand and navigate difference. Multicultural service-learning initiatives have the potential to shift abstract principles of multiculturalism to a real-world and relevant context with implications for social change.

References

Astin, A. W., Vogelgesang, L. J., Ikeda, E. K., and Yee, J. A. *How Service Learning Affects Students.* Los Angeles: Higher Education Research Institute, UCLA, 2000.

Boyle-Baise, M. *Multicultural Service Learning: Educating Teachers in Diverse Communities.* New York: Teachers College Press, 2002.

Butin, D. W. "The Limits of Service-Learning in Higher Education." *The Review of Higher Education,* 2006, 29(4), 473–498.

Butin, D. W. *Service-Learning and Social Justice Education: Strengthening Justice-Oriented Community Based Models of Teaching and Learning.* London: Routledge, 2008.

Campus Compact. *Who We Are.* 2013. Retrieved June 15, 2013, from http://www.compact.org/about/history-mission-vision/

Cipolle, S. B. *Service-Learning and Social Justice: Engaging Students in Social Change.* Lanham, Md.: Rowman & Littlefield Publishers, 2010.

Donahue, D. M. "The Nature of Teaching and Learning Dilemmas." In C. Cress, D. Donahue, and Associates (eds.), *Democratic Dilemmas of Teaching Service-Learning: Curricular Strategies for Success.* Sterling, Va.: Stylus Publishing, 2011.

Eby, J. W. *Why Service-Learning Is Bad.* 1998. Retrieved June 15, 2013, from http://www.servicelearning.org/library/resource/4703

Endres, D., and Gould, M. "'I Am Also in the Position to Use My Whiteness to Help Them Out': The Communication of Whiteness in Service Learning." *Western Journal of Communication,* 2009, 73(4), 418–436.

Eyler, J., Giles, D. E., Jr., Stenson, C. M., and Gray, C. J. *At a Glance: What We Know About the Effects of Service-Learning on College Students, Faculty, Institutions and Communities, 1993–2000.* 3rd ed. Nashville, Tenn.: Vanderbilt University, 2001.

Illich, I. "To Hell with Good Intentions." In A. Gilvin, G. M. Roberts, and C. Martin (eds.), *Collaborative Futures: Critical Reflections on Publicly Active Graduate Education.* Syracuse, N.Y.: The Graduate School Press of Syracuse University, 2012.

Komives, S. R. "Increasing Student Involvement through Civic Leadership Education." In C. C. Schroeder, P. Mable, and Associates (eds.), *Realizing the Educational Potential of College Residence Halls.* San Francisco: Jossey-Bass, 1994.

Mitchell, D. T. "Traditional vs. Critical Service-Learning: Engaging the Literature to Differentiate Two Models." *Michigan Journal of Community Service Learning,* 2008a, 14(2), 50–65.

Mitchell, D. T. "Critical Service-Learning as Social Justice Education: A Case Study of the Citizen Scholars Program." In D. Butin (ed.), *Service-Learning and Social Justice Education: Strengthening Justice-Oriented Community Based Models of Teaching and Learning.* London: Routledge, 2008b.

O'Grady, C. R. (ed.). *Integrating Service Learning and Multicultural Education in Colleges and Universities.* Mahwah, N.J.: L. Erlbaum Associates, 2000.

Rhoads, R. A. *Community Service and Higher Learning: Explorations of the Caring Self.* Albany: State University of New York Press, 1997.

Rice, K., and Pollack, S. "Developing a Critical Pedagogy of Service Learning: Preparing Self-Reflective, Culturally Aware, and Responsive Community Participants." In C. O'Grady (ed.), *Integrating Service Learning and Multicultural Education in Colleges and Universities.* Mahwah, N.J.: L. Erlbaum Associates, 2000.

Seider, S. C., and Hillman, A. "Challenging Privileged College Students' Othering Language in Community Service Learning." *Journal of College and Character,* 2011, 12(3), 1–7.

Sperling, R. "Service-Learning as a Method of Teaching Multiculturalism to White College Students." *Journal of Latinos and Education,* 2007, 6(4), 309–322.

Watt, S. K. "Difficult Dialogues, Privilege and Social Justice: Uses of the Privileged Identity Exploration (PIE) Model in Student Affairs Practice." *College Student Affairs Journal,* 2007, 26(2), 114–126.

Watt, S. K. "Moving Beyond the Talk: From Difficult Dialogue to Action." In J. Arminio, V. Torres, and R. Pope (eds.), *Why Aren't We There Yet? Taking Personal Responsibility for Creating an Inclusive Campus.* Sterling, Va.: Stylus Publishing, 2011.

Weah, W., Cornelia, V., and Hall, M. "Service-Learning and Multicultural/Multiethnic Perspectives." *Phi Delta Kappan*, 2000, *81*, 673–675.

KIRA PASQUESI *is a doctoral student in the Higher Education and Student Affairs program at the University of Iowa.*

New Directions for Student Services • DOI: 10.1002/ss

Student SEED (Seeking Educational Equity and Diversity) is a grassroots, social justice course in which participants actively engage in dialogue about diversity and social identity. This chapter examines Student SEED as a multicultural initiative.

5

Who I Am Is the Text. Who I Become Is the Purpose

Heidi Arbisi-Kelm, Jasmine P. Clay, Mariko M. Lin, Rodney Horikawa, William H. Clifton, Seema Kapani

Students who engage with peers in diversity-related, interactional experiences demonstrate gains in problem solving (Chang, 1999), active and collaborative learning (Terenzini, Cabrera, Colbeck, Bjorklund, and Parente, 2001), and consideration of multiple perspectives (Gurin, Dey, Gurin, and Hurtado, 2003). These learning outcomes are valued by future employers and in a democratic society, but how do institutions actively foster opportunities for students to engage across difference, and what principles should guide these efforts? This chapter profiles a successful, grassroots, social justice dialogue course, Student SEED (Seeking Educational Equity and Diversity), by examining its essential elements.

Student SEED's Essential Elements

Student SEED is a multicultural initiative that helps undergraduate students build their capacity for engaging with difference in a diverse society. During each class, Student SEED participants actively engage in dialogue about race and ethnicity, religion, sexual identity, ability, socio-economic status, the gender spectrum, allyship, and how social identities intersect. The goal of SEED is to cultivate educationally purposeful interactions among students in order that they may develop multicultural competence and critical social consciousness.

For ten years, one or two sections of SEED have been taught each semester at the University of Wisconsin–Madison. SEED, which was adapted for higher education from the Wellesley Centers for Women National SEED Project on Inclusive Curriculum, is not a required course, is open to all majors, and is most commonly taken by sophomores and

NEW DIRECTIONS FOR STUDENT SERVICES, no. 144, Winter 2013 © 2013 Wiley Periodicals, Inc.
Published online in Wiley Online Library (wileyonlinelibrary.com) • DOI: 10.1002/ss.20068

juniors. Classes are limited to twenty-five students and offered for academic credit. Most often scheduled through the College of Letters and Science, SEED has also been sponsored by other schools within the university such as education, engineering, business, and the health sciences. The design and implementation of SEED is influenced by many factors; however, the following essential elements lay the groundwork for designing and implementing a dialogue course as an effective multicultural initiative. SEED's essential elements are its conceptual foundation, course composition, instructional team, and curriculum.

SEED's Conceptual Foundation.   Three footings serve as the base for SEED's conceptual foundation: understanding and dismantling oppression, dialogue, and first-person learning.

Understanding and Dismantling Oppression.   In the first chapter of this volume, Watt presents two conceptual lenses that can be used to frame multicultural initiatives: diversity as a "social good" and diversity as a "social value" (Watt, 2011, p. 132; Watt, Chapter 1 of this volume). Stemming from a desire to teach cultural competency *and* critical thinking related to social stratification, current and historical inequality, and the social constructs that favor majority identities and subjugate marginalized ones, SEED pedagogy is solidly grounded in the concept of diversity as a social value. As a social justice education course, SEED aims for nothing less than personal, institutional, and societal transformation. Cultural competency is an aspect of this, but it is only one part. SEED's ultimate purpose is to develop culturally competent citizens who will interrupt oppression and ignite transformative social change.

The following example illustrates the way in which SEED is organized around the concept of diversity as a value. Instead of working to *teach tolerance* across the gender spectrum—that is, among men, women, and cisgendered–transgendered individuals—SEED strives to broaden students' perspectives and prepare them to critically frame and challenge sexism, transphobia, and hegemony. The former (teaching tolerance) is an example of diversity as a social good and the latter is an example of diversity as a social value. The difference can be explained this way: diversity as a social good is a limited approach that requires only a "surface level" (Watt, Chapter 1 of this volume) commitment to diversity. Participants of these types of multicultural initiatives merely ensure that historically marginalized groups are included without necessarily questioning the structural social paradigms that lead to their exclusion. Multicultural initiatives organized around the concept of diversity as a social good often function in alignment with "cultural norms" and may perpetuate inequity between marginalized and privileged groups (Watt, Chapter 1 of this volume). Conversely, SEED participants take steps toward the goal of inclusion by embarking on a deeply personal and self-reflective journey. It is an experience during which they are supported and challenged to examine their perspectives on diversity and to develop skills for building a critical understanding of systemic oppression.

To foster deep learning about social justice, SEED facilitators work to plant *seeds* of dissonance for students. Through experiential course activities and conversations, students' personal biases and perceptions, which may have previously gone unnoticed, come to the surface. The intention is to help students consider the social identity lenses through which they have come to view the world. The closed fishbowl exercise provides an example of how this is done. The closed fishbowl is a class activity in which a select group of students holds a conversation while a larger group listens. Dialogues held among students selected into a fishbowl because of shared, privileged, social identity characteristics are revealing. Often students' limitations related to communicating their ideas about privilege are immediately apparent. Many students struggle to articulate thoughts about their shared, agent, social identity—especially in the presence of students from target identities. Therefore, while teaching respect (tolerance) for diverse viewpoints is a course aim, the aspirational goal of SEED is to facilitate a basic understanding of privilege and to prepare students with skills to effectively navigate difference and challenge injustice. A semester in the SEED course can lead to moments of confusion, humility, and struggle, but it can also be nothing short of transformational.

Dialogue.   If social justice education functions as the soil for SEED classroom learning, participant dialogue acts as the primary tool of instruction. Bringing diverse individuals together "to talk and learn from each other" (Zúñiga, 2003, p. 8) is one way to help students foster relationships across difference and build the capacity to take action for social change. Arising from the premise that students' most important teachers are other students (Chickering, 1969), SEED is designed to develop a community engaged in difficult dialogue. A "difficult dialogue" is defined as an exchange of ideas that "centers on an awakening of potentially conflicting views ... about social justice issues" (Watt, 2007, p. 116). SEED facilitators create a classroom environment in which participants gain deeper personal insight by taking risks and challenging themselves and others to discuss difficult topics.

Consequently, while SEED utilizes multiple modalities of teaching and learning—including assigned readings, in-class videos, and reflective writing—its central teaching tools are the continued meaningful conversations and, often challenging, interactions that occur among participants in and outside the classroom. In students' words, this approach "creates space" for learning about themselves and others. SEED subscribes to the notion that sustained dialogue provides the opportunity for authentic expression related to examining sociopolitical issues, social identity, socially constructed power imbalances, and group differences (Zúñiga, 2003). Through dialogue, SEED participants discuss their agent and target identities, and they reflect on how their social identities relate to and interact with those of their classmates. Across the semester, the SEED classroom becomes a place where students engage in sustained conversation about difference to raise their awareness, question privilege, and help lead campus from a culture of assimilation and structural exclusion toward one of authentic inclusion and balanced social power.

First-Person Learning.   The last footing of SEED's conceptual foundation is first-person learning. SEED uses "the textbooks of our lives" (McIntosh, 2004) as the instructional curriculum. SEED classes are organized around personal sharing and students' "lived experience" (Bell, 1997). Using this approach, SEED participants examine issues of privilege and oppression not merely through academic textbooks but from the rich textbooks of their unique identities and experiences. In Chapter 1, Watt underscores the value of pursuing an inward journey toward engaging with difference. Unlike multicultural initiatives that mandate us to open *our* campus environments to the presence of *the other*, SEED initiates inclusion by inviting us to start with ourselves. SEED participants are asked to raise their awareness about their internal processes, for example, initial reactions, deepest feelings, and candid thoughts, as they engage with diverse others. By grounding the structure and content of each class in students' personal experience, their unique stories shape and direct their—and their classmates'—discovery and development. By mining and sharing their own rich histories, students learn about the broader topics of social identity diversity and its impact.

Locating learning in students' experience also fosters a classroom environment that validates learners as knowers and defines learning as mutually constructed meaning (Baxter Magolda, 2004; Davidson, 2011). *Pedagogy of the Oppressed* (Freire, 1970) was an inspiration for SEED founders. In accord with a Freirean approach, there is no one expert telling SEED participants what they need to learn. Instead, students co-create the classroom and curriculum. A former SEED participant says, "the emphasis on the self is the most essential. So much of what we study in other courses focuses ... on this objective truth ... but SEED challenges the students to think about themselves and trust their own experiences" (communication with authors, January 9, 2013).

By inviting lived experiences and self-directed learning into the classroom, SEED provides opportunities for students to share with and learn from each other, first-hand, about social identity diversity and social justice as it relates to their own lives. This prepares students to understand systematic oppression by examining their role as both an agent and a target of privilege, and teaches them that the responsibility for justice is shared by both those historically privileged and marginalized (Watt, Chapter 1 of this volume). Compelling students to actively study themselves and direct their own learning subverts a diversity education approach that allows students to be passive recipients of knowledge about the other. Instead, SEED participants must look in the mirror and make active choices about who they want to be in relation to difference.

Intentional Course Composition.   "Start with the end in mind" is a truism for good teaching. While any UW-Madison student is eligible to enroll in SEED, course registration is managed through an application process. College students who engage in interactions with peers who are different from them show a greater openness to diverse perspectives and a willingness to challenge their own beliefs (Pascarella, Edison, Nora, Hagedorn, and Terenzini, 1996). Accordingly, SEED class cohorts are intentionally composed to reflect a broad spectrum of diverse social identities. The SEED objective of facilitating conditions under which students engage with difference is well served by this approach. SEED participants report that during class they interact with peers they might never otherwise have met, expand their perspective, and gain exposure to alternative viewpoints.

Instructional Team.   SEED's educational model and course instruction rely on a facilitator team, each of whom is selected to represent a range of diverse identities, backgrounds, and expertise areas. The facilitation team's main purpose is to support students' understanding and expression of their personal experiences while also helping them develop the ability to critically frame societal norms and unconscious biases. The team approach serves several purposes: first, multiple facilitators who represent diverse and intersecting social identities can serve as a model of engaging with difference and difficult dialogue. When others lead by example, engaging with difference—and the associated conflict that may result—can come to be viewed by students as a "positive practice" (Watt, Chapter 1 of this volume), that is, one that is productive and transformative. Second, given the multiple and various social identities of the SEED participants, individual students may identify with some facilitator(s) more than others. While students are assigned to a small group led by a single instructor, it is explicit that students are welcome to engage with all members of the instructional team. Also, while each SEED facilitator is skilled in managing difficult dialogues, there are common expressions of resistance or "defense modes" (Watt, 2007, p. 114) that students may display as they learn about privilege and oppression. Student learning may be most effective if a facilitator from a privileged identity highlights and addresses the microaggressions that occur in class. In addition, the SEED program recognizes that supporting students' identity development related to privilege is hard work. SEED facilitators have witnessed how one loaded statement can require an entire session to unpack. Like SEED participants, SEED facilitators may be triggered by students' comments (Griffin, 1997). The team facilitation model allows for instructors to exchange which of them leads conversations as they evolve. This can help each facilitator be most effective in the classroom. Finally, SEED facilitators also have privileged identities, and privilege doesn't always *see* itself well. The facilitation team is diverse and expected to support and challenge each other's growth and development. An example is the way in which SEED has historically handled conversations about gender. Until recently, SEED participants were guided to explore the topic of gender with exercises oriented around male and female experiences. However, facilitators realized that the practice of gender as binary was exclusive. Consequently, the SEED program has completely restructured class sessions that cover gender. Ultimately, SEED facilitators are guiding students' journeys, but as facilitators encourage students to become more deeply aware of privilege and act against injustice, we acknowledge that we must expect the same from ourselves.

SEED Curriculum.   Below is a brief description of the curricular components of the program.

Learning through Reflection.   Through personal reflection, SEED participants raise their awareness, understanding, and development of their social identities. SEED is designed to foster reflection across every activity, conversation, and assignment; however, the primary tool used to encourage learning through personal reflection is the weekly journal assignment. Journal reflections serve as a means for students to process their thoughts and feelings related to topics such as intersecting identities, privilege, discrimination, and opportunities to act against injustice. They also facilitate the essential element of a sustained dialogue on diversity. SEED participants report that this type of extended conversation about diversity isn't something that occurs in other classes. Through ongoing, personal reflection, SEED participants synthesize their experiences and demonstrate what they learn. They gain insight into how their social identities shape their interactions and also have the chance to reimagine who they can become.

Community.   An expansive word, community is essential to SEED work in myriad ways. One goal for this volume is to fill practitioners' toolkits with useful ideas. Here we share two exercises that are used by SEED facilitators to help build community and relationships among course participants.

Building a community for honest and meaningful sharing is imperative to the success of a social justice dialogue course because creating a culture of risk-taking is a necessary first step in the work of self-examination, understanding privilege, building empathy, and forging a personal commitment to take action for social change. Each SEED class begins with an *opening*, which is a moment when a participant—a facilitator or a student—shares something personal. This could be a story, a keepsake, or a talent relating to participants' cultural background, lived experience, or a salient social identity. During openings, SEED participants often share something that is deeply meaningful to them. Openings thus become a means for the sharer to let others know they value and trust the SEED community. Reciprocally, the SEED community demonstrates respect and value for its peer by receiving that which is shared. What results is a classroom environment that is enriched by the unique character of each SEED participant and a learning community that is prepared to journey together.

NEW DIRECTIONS FOR STUDENT SERVICES • DOI: 10.1002/ss

Common Ground is an activity that helps SEED participants identify similarities within the group and get to know one another. From a
facilitator perspective, this activity may also provide valuable information
about the experiences and social identities of the current class cohort. Students are asked to form a large circle with everyone facing inward. Facilitators verbalize statements such as "I feel like I belong on campus." Students
are asked to consider whether the statements apply to them, and step into
the circle if they do apply. Others remain in their place. Everyone is encouraged to be observant and take notice of their classmates' responses. After
approximately ten facilitator-led statements, students are invited to vocal-
ize statements that are true of themselves. Thus, common ground provides
students an intentional means to "make a statement" among their peers
and to feel validated when others step into the circle to share the common
ground on which they stand together. To further build community, facilitators also participate in the circle and, afterward, the class debriefs their
reactions.

Connecting Awareness to Action.   The final essential element of SEED
as a multicultural initiative is the curricular component of connecting
awareness to action. In Chapter 1 of this volume, Watt recommends that
multicultural initiatives that organize around the concept of "diversity
as a value" pair dialogue with action. We conclude this chapter by describing two activities that we have used to help SEED participants with
consciousness-raising and allyship development.

Closed Fishbowls are an opportunity for a select group of students to
engage in dialogue while the rest of the class observes quietly. Often, the
selected group shares a social identity feature or characteristic, but not always. For this activity, the selected group forms a circle in the middle of the
room and the rest of the class sits outside the inner circle. During the dialogue, the outside group cannot talk or contribute to the conversation. After
a designated amount of time, the group on the outside is given the opportunity to share their observations with the larger group. This is an effective
activity for raising consciousness among students both inside and outside
of the circle. Students report that this activity helps them be accountable to
each other and recognize their *covered spots* or the ways in which their privilege is invisible to them. An important consideration for this activity is to
start the exercise by inviting the agent identity group into the dialogue circle first. This encourages them to focus on issues related to privilege instead
of discussing the conversation just held by the target-identity group.

Stages of Allyship is an activity that uses "Coming Out as a Straight
Ally" adapted from the Human Rights Campaign Foundation by Ladelle
McWhorter (1996). It is planned for the final course sessions in order to
help students connect awareness to action. Students are provided with a
stack of different colored post-it notes. Each color corresponds to an identity discussed during the semester. Students are asked to anonymously rank
themselves as an ally of each social identity group by assigning a number

to each post-it note. The notes are then hung up on the wall as a visual representation of allyship for the class. It is powerful to see how students rate their allyship across different identities and where the highest rankings reside. During the large group debrief, students often discuss what it means to be an ally. They pose questions to each other such as "Who determines if one is an ally?"; "Is it possible to be ally to every identity?"; and "How can I work to recognize my privilege in the hope of being a better ally to others?"

Conclusion

Numerous challenges face a multicultural initiative like SEED: (1) organizers must secure an academic home and funding for the course, (2) the team-teaching model is capital intensive and time consuming, and (3) the emphasis on learning through dialogue and personal experience can position the course in opposition to the established pedagogy of academia. Nonetheless, SEED participants report that the class frequently serves as their first opportunity to examine their social identity on a personal level within a critical framework. The SEED classroom community cultivates a learning posture of honesty, attentive listening, the ability to self-reflect, and respect for one another's right to be heard. According to a former participant, "SEED was the first time in my life where I had no choice but to talk about oppression and realize how my identities might play a factor in someone else's oppression or exclusion, whether I am aware of it or not" (communication with the authors, January 6, 2013).

Through multicultural initiatives such as SEED, colleges and universities create meaningful opportunities for students to engage across difference. Intentional and "difficult" dialogues can lead to greater personal and social awareness. We submit SEED as an example of a multicultural initiative that compels students and the greater campus community to shift the values, structure, and politics of the university environment. With the hope of creating a more inclusive and socially just society, SEED serves to develop good citizens who value difference and take their lessons learned inside the classroom into their journey beyond it.

References

Baxter Magolda, M. B. "Create Learning Partnerships in Higher Education: Modeling the Shape, Shaping the Model." In M. B. Baxter Magolda and P. M. King (eds.), *Learning Partnerships: Theory and Models of Practice to Educate for Self-Authorship*. Sterling, Va.: Stylus, 2004.

Bell, L. A. "Theoretical Foundations for Social Justice Education." In M. Adams, L. A. Bell, and P. Griffin (eds.), *Teachings for Diversity and Social Justice: A Sourcebook*. New York: Routledge, 1997.

Chang, M. J. "Does Racial Diversity Matter? The Educational Impact of a Racially Diverse Undergraduate Population." *Journal of College Student Development*, 1999, *40*, 377–395.

Chickering, A. W. *Education and Identity*. San Francisco: Jossey-Bass, 1969.

Davidson, D. "Tale Teaching Tip #2: Self-Authorship & the Learning Partnership Model." *Teaching and Learning Enhancement Center*, Bloomsburg University of Pennsylvania, 2011. Retrieved November 15, 2012, from http://orgs.bloomu.edu /tale/documents/TT_2_SelfAuthorship.pdf

Freire, P. *Pedagogy of the Oppressed*. New York: Continuum, 1970.

Griffin, P. "Introductory Module for the Single Issue Courses." In M. Adams, L. A. Bell, and P. Griffin (eds.), *Teachings for Diversity and Social Justice: A Sourcebook*. New York: Routledge, 1997.

Gurin, P., Dey, E., Gurin, G., and Hurtado, S. "How Does Racial/Ethnic Diversity Promote Education?" *Western Journal of Black Studies*, 2003, 27(1), 20–29.

McIntosh, P. "Empowering Educators Through SEED: An Interview with Peggy McIntosh." *Research and Action Report*, 2004, 25(2), 10–15.

McWhorter, L. "Coming Out as a Straight Ally." *Human Rights Campaign Foundation*, 1996. Retrieved from http://www.uas.alaska.edu/juneau/activities/safezone /docs/straight_ally.pdf

Pascarella, E. T., Edison, M., Nora, A., Hagedorn, L. S., and Terenzini, P. T. "Influences on Students' Openness to Diversity and Challenge in the First Year of College." *Journal of Higher Education*, 1996, 67(2), 174–195.

Terenzini, P. T., Cabrera, A. F., Colbeck, C. L., Bjorklund, S. A., and Parente, J. M. "Racial and Ethnic Diversity in the Classroom: Does it Promote Student Learning?" *Journal of Higher Education*, 2001, 72(5), 509–531.

Watt, S. K. "Difficult Dialogues, Privilege and Social Justice: Uses of the Privileged Identity Exploration (PIE) Model in Student Affairs Practice." *College Student Affairs Journal*, 2007, 26(2), 114–126.

Watt, S. K. "Moving Beyond the Talk." In J. Arminio, V. Torres, and R. L. Pope (eds.), *Why Aren't We There Yet?: Taking Personal Responsibility for Creating an Inclusive Campus*. Sterling, Va.: Stylus, 2011.

Zúñiga, X. "Bridging Differences through Dialogue." *About Campus*, 2003, 7(6), 8–16.

HEIDI ARBISI-KELM, JASMINE P. CLAY, MARIKO M. LIN, RODNEY HORIKAWA, WILLIAM H. CLIFTON, AND SEEMA KAPANI *are current or former University of Wisconsin–Madison Student SEED course facilitators.*

NEW DIRECTIONS FOR STUDENT SERVICES • DOI: 10.1002/ss

6

This chapter briefly overviews the Principles and Practices of the Circle of Trust® approach and shares an example of how those ideals informed how an instructor team facilitated a multiculturalism in higher education and student affairs course.

Courage in Multicultural Initiatives

Sherry K. Watt, Margaret Golden,
Lisa A. P. Schumacher, Luis S. Moreno

If the goal of multicultural initiatives is to transform our institutional structures to allow for more equitable opportunities and outcomes, providing a safe space that encourages authentic participation and honest exploration is essential. The Principles and Practices of the Circle of Trust® approach provides a framework for creating such a space. This space is particularly important when discussing, for example, race, gender, sexual orientation, culture, and outlook because issues such as these touch on the very notion of who we are and what we value. These are issues of the heart. In *Healing the Heart of Democracy: The Courage to Create a Politics Worthy of the Human Spirit*, Parker Palmer (2011, p. 10) describes the heart this way:

> [T]he heart is where everything begins: that grounded place in us where we can overcome fear, rediscover that we are members of one another, and embrace the conflicts that threaten democracy as openings to new life for us and for our nation.

The Principles and Practices of the Circle of Trust® approach were developed by Parker Palmer and others at the Center for Courage & Renewal to "invite groups into a communal process ... through which we engage our deepest questions in a way that welcomes our inwardness even as it connects us to the gifts and challenges of community and to the larger world" (Chadsey and Jackson, 2012, p. 4). What follows is a discussion of the principles and practices that have particular salience for the exploration within multicultural initiatives. Authors share insights gained from teaching a course entitled Multiculturalism in Higher Education and Student Affairs using the Circle of Trust® approach.

New Directions for Student Services, no. 144, Winter 2013 © 2013 Wiley Periodicals, Inc.
Published online in Wiley Online Library (wileyonlinelibrary.com) • DOI: 10.1002/ss.20069

Principles and Practices of the Circle of Trust® Approach

The Center for Courage and Renewal embraces diversity as a core value. It states: "Diversity is a deeply valued source of strength, richness and wisdom for us and for the communities in which we live and work. The capacity to welcome and make space for diverse voices and multiple perspectives is critical to the creation of Circles of Trust® and to the healing and wholeness needed in our world" (Center for Courage & Renewal, 2013, "Our Core Values," para. 3). The mission of the Center for Courage and Renewal is "to nurture personal and professional integrity and the courage to act on it" (Chadsey and Jackson, 2012, p. 11). While the focus of the Center's work is broad, these principles and practices are naturally transferable and provide a unique container to support effective implementation of a wide range of multicultural initiatives. Below are the key principles and practices of the Circle of Trust® approach that are relevant to the design and implementation of multicultural initiatives.

Key Principles of the Circle of Trust® Approach

The Circle of Trust® Approach assumes that the exploration of any complex issue requires an inner examination of one's values, beliefs, and ways of being in the world. A few key principles underlie this approach. They include that this inner journeying requires both solitude and community; that there is profound utility in exploring paradox; and that there is a hidden wholeness available despite the brokenness we experience in the world.

Inner Work Requires Solitude and Community. In Circles of Trust®, we make space for the solitude that allows us to learn from within, while supporting that solitude with the resources of community. Participants take an inner journey in community where we learn how to evoke and challenge each other without being judgmental, directive, or invasive.

Our country's history of institutional racism has created a legacy of privilege for some and lack of opportunity for others. In addition, it has left all of us deeply wounded by our separation from one another. Through dialogue in spaces free from judgment, neither evasive nor invasive, we can relearn our connectedness and begin to reform our institutions. College campuses have historically been fertile ground for deeper exploration of culture. Applying this key principle shifts the weight and role of direct confrontations that are often par for the course when engaging in dialogue around controversial issues. At the same time, the high value of holding oneself accountable to one's own wounds and inflictions creates a space where authentic, critical, and in-depth personal as well as collective exploration of social oppression can take place.

NEW DIRECTIONS FOR STUDENT SERVICES • DOI: 10.1002/ss

An Appreciation of Paradox Enriches Our Lives and Helps Us Hold Greater Complexity.   The journey we take in a Circle of Trust® teaches us to approach the many polarities that come with being human as "both–ands" rather than "either–ors," holding them in ways that open us to new insights and possibilities. We listen to the inner teacher and to the voices in the circle, letting our own insights and the wisdom that can emerge in conversation check and balance each other. We trust both our intellects and the knowledge that comes through our bodies, intuitions, and emotions.

When we explore our different realities through the lens of paradox, we can embrace other perspectives without the fear of losing ourselves in the process. This frees us from clinging to the "rightness" of our own ideas and allows us to respond to the other with compassion and creativity rather than polarization and fear. This volume defines *Difference* as having dissimilar opinions, experiences, ideologies, epistemologies, and/or constructions of reality about self, society, and/or identity. College students are extremely malleable when they first arrive to a higher education institution. They have to learn skills to manage paradoxes. How well one manages conflict related to *Difference* is an essential skill set for living in diverse societies. For example, a first-year college student raised in one religious value system is likely going to encounter another student from a different faith tradition and each may differ on how they view certain issues, such as the role of males versus females in the home, contraception/birth control, or abortion/right to life. Part of the college experience is to engage in dialogue with others who have different views. Through high-impact experiences inside and outside the classroom, educators aim to increase students' knowledge, skills, and awareness (Pope, Reynolds, and Mueller, 2004) related to both their discipline of study and also these types of differences.

A "Hidden Wholeness" Underlies Our Lives.   Whatever brokenness we experience in ourselves and in the world, a "hidden wholeness" can be found just beneath the surface. The capacity to stand and act with integrity in the gap between what is and what could be or should be—resisting both the corrosive cynicism that comes from seeing only what is broken and the irrelevant idealism that comes from seeing only what is not—has been key to every life-giving movement and is among the fruits of the Circle of Trust® approach. Keeping in mind this principle creates a unique space where facilitators can engage groups in difficult dialogues around *Difference* while trusting that individuals have the capacity to embrace their own wholeness as they are also honoring the experiences of others that are different from themselves.

As we continue to bring new multicultural initiatives forward, it will require that we develop the capacity to hold the tension inherent in the gap between our present state, for example, of race relations and our visions for the future. We must continue to acknowledge that which is broken, in our hearts and our institutions, and recognize the hidden wholeness available to all of us when we act with integrity to change the things we can. These key principles of the Circle of Trust® approach can be used to guide multicultural initiatives. Next, we share some specific practices that facilitators use to enact these principles.

Key Practices of the Circle of Trust® Approach

There are three key practices of this signature approach that are relevant for multicultural initiatives. Those include no fixing, advising, "saving," or correcting one another; asking honest and open questions; and using multiple modes of reflection.

Committing to No Fixing, Advising, "Saving," or Correcting One Another.   Everything we do is guided by this simple rule, one that honors the primacy and integrity of the inner teacher. When we are free from external judgment, we are more likely to have an honest conversation with ourselves and learn to check and correct ourselves from within.

This commitment creates a space where participants can speak their truth without fear of judgment or reprisal, then listen carefully to the truth of others who speak. Given this self-corrective approach, participants are more likely to wrestle with disparities in what they hear, see things anew, and assimilate new knowledge and understanding into their own perspectives.

Asking Honest, Open Questions to "Hear Each Other into Speech." Instead of advising each other, we learn to listen deeply and ask questions that help others hear their own inner wisdom more clearly. As we learn to ask questions that are not advice in disguise, that have no other purpose than to help someone listen to the inner teacher, all of us learn and grow.

The experience of not being heard or understood can keep people trapped in their own experience, not willing to reconsider their viewpoints for fear of giving up a part of themselves. Using honest, open questions creates a new form of listening, one intended to help the speaker hear their own inner dialogue, without the advice or admonishment of others to get in their way. This listening allows for new insights, observations of stated contradictions, and opportunities for the speaker to internalize new learning about self, the other, and the nature of reality.

Using Multiple Modes of Reflection So Everyone Can Find His or Her Place and Pace.   In Circles of Trust®, we speak and we listen. We explore important questions in large group conversation and dialogues in small groups. We make time for individual reflection and journaling. We respect nonverbal ways of learning, including music, movement, and the arts. We honor the educative power of silence and the healing power of laughter. Together we weave a "tapestry of truth" with many and diverse threads, creating a pattern in which everyone can find a place that both affirms and stretches them.

NEW DIRECTIONS FOR STUDENT SERVICES • DOI: 10.1002/ss

This practice exemplifies what it means to truly honor the experience of others. When we create space that celebrates our differences, we begin to see how our lives are diminished when one of us is absent from the conversation. Paradoxically, the more we make room in the conversation for diverse voices and perspectives, the more opportunities we have to appreciate the similarities inherent in our human experience. This appreciation can lead to connection, empathy, and understanding, a good place from which to grow. The Circle of Trust® approach gives students a safe place where they can imagine a society where everyone is responsible for eradicating social oppression within education, employment, or social settings. These practices help facilitators to create a space where each student can safely and critically make meaning of the role race, gender, religion, sex, and sexual orientation in the context of the human experience.

Uses of the Circle of Trust® Principles and Practices: Teaching Multiculturalism in Higher Education and Student Affairs

A main goal of higher education is to foster student development and learning that provides the potential for effective citizenship and lifelong growth (Torres, 2011). A course for higher education and student affairs professionals training to work on college campuses needs to promote general growth and increase capacity for new professionals to manage *Difference* so that they can foster that same skill development for students that they will work with in the future. The course being described below aimed to use the Circle of Trust® approach to develop the skills for managing *Difference* more effectively. Next, we will *introduce the instructor team*, the *philosophical tensions* explored by the team, and finally share *a unique classroom activity* that exemplifies how the Circle of Trust® approach can provide a perfect container to support effective implementation of a multicultural initiative.

Introducing the Instructor Team.   This course was taught by an instructor team of three that included an African American female faculty member with over fifteen years of experience in teaching multiculturalism courses (Sherry); a third-year white, female doctoral student with limited teaching experience in multiculturalism at the higher education level but who has worked with people from marginalized populations as a recreational therapist (Lisa); and a Latino, male doctoral candidate in his final year of the program with personal, research, and professional experiences in exploring social oppression (Luis).

Sherry intentionally chose a diverse instructor team to facilitate a class of twenty students from different geographical parts of the world and varying in age, race, sex, sexual orientation, and abilities. Sherry, Lisa, and Luis brought different perspectives to the instructor team, which enriched our course preparation discussions that allowed us to create an environment with a wide range of instructional strategies to serve our diverse group of students. For instance, Lisa spent twenty years as a recreational therapist and a massage therapist. In addition to being a police officer, Luis has held numerous positions in higher education including being an assistant director of multicultural services within student activities. The instructor team applied the principles in practices of Circle of Trust® work to create a safe space to share their own discomfort about the content and what it felt like to engage in these discussions from both marginalized and privileged positions. As bell hooks states, "There must be an ongoing recognition that everyone influences the classroom dynamic that everyone contributes" (hooks, 1994, p. 8).

"Practicing" these dialogues as an instructor team was a significant component of our class preparation and informed how we designed our curriculum and interacted with the class. The personal relationships we developed as a diverse and supportive instructor team allowed our individual teaching styles to comfortably emerge in the classroom.

Using the Circle of Trust® Approach: Philosophical Tensions. Multicultural education focuses "on social identity, sociocultural and historical context, and community-based experiments for change" (Adams, Bell, and Griffin, 2007, p. 24). The instructor team had an appreciation for the fact that through this course students were supposed to learn more about power and inequity within our society. As is the case with any sixteen-week course, waiting for students to experience the "aha" moment in respect of multicultural teaching at their own speed can be exasperating. We found ourselves wanting to make sure the students left the class with an appreciation and understanding of how those not in the privileged majority had experiences that were real and at times "ugly." The instructors also wrestled with philosophical differences we held as it related to the utility of the role of stress juxtapose with positive emotions when exploring controversial issues. We questioned whether creating too much stress would push them "over the edge" and wondered if allowing too much positive emotion would "let them off the hook." Our teaching team wrestled with how to balance the Circle of Trust® approach with our desires to guide the process with more intention. We questioned at times the invitational nature of the approach juxtapose with the fact that this was a course with required reading, experiential, and writing assignments all for a grade. While we managed these tensions weekly during our instructor team meetings as well as in class, we were pleasantly surprised to find that we did not lose some of these aspects in the teaching process.

In fact, we observed ways the Circle of Trust® approach allowed space for many different learning styles. For example, we feared that students who did not participate fully in classroom discussion and appear as if they were not reading the assignments were passing up an opportunity to expand their minds and skill development. In reality, many of the students were simply embracing another tenet of the Circle of Trust®, which speaks to *what is offered in the circle is by invitation, not demand* (Golden, 2012). These students often surprised the instructor team by showing their mastery of the subject matter in their writing assignments.

The Circle of Trust® approach, our personal teaching styles, and our lived experiences all sat together at the core of the classroom management. Students faced the different ways we viewed the world. For example, Luis facilitated learning within urgency and intensity. He wanted the students to understand how these limitations especially affected the lives of marginalized groups and also wanted to inspire the students to take action. We listened to each other and infused more directed experiences at times. These exchanges created a healthy tension within the instructor team that tested the boundaries of the container created by the principles and practices of Circles of Trust®. Ultimately, our instructor team concluded that our different teaching styles gave the students the "real-world" exposure to different approaches and created an additional lesson about the process for students that partnered the content. All of these aspects worked together to encourage skill development for engaging *Difference*.

Multicultural social justice education was often the base from which discussion occurred in the class (Sleeter and Grant, 2008). We held up and examined the distribution of limited goods and resources based on principles of equity, need, or equality. This way of engaging difference communicated a shared responsibility between those who are marginalized and privileged. In other words, our class discussions leaned more in the direction of no longer being about one group receiving something based on their race, color, gender, religion, and sexuality. Rather, we critically examined ways that opportunities to succeed in our society are differently experienced based on your identity.

Ultimately, the Circle of Trust® approach created more space for students to do deeper work around social oppression with a lesser intensity of blame and shame that is usually present within typical multicultural education courses. And we eventually decided to educate students on the theory behind stress and positive emotions as a part of the curriculum. Next, we will share the classroom activity and briefly describe the theoretical idea that exemplifies reactions to stress and the utility of positive emotions in learning.

Using the Circle of Trust® Approach: A Unique Classroom Activity. Holding true to the Principles and Practices of the Circle of Trust® approach fostered within the instructor team the value of creating learning experiences on the slant. The instructor team crafted a unique activity that embraced the Circle of Trust® approach by including activities that welcomed storytelling through the use of poetry and metaphor to examine critical issues. The activity described below was situated among many experiences where students were invited to participate in opportunities such as hearing the story of and engaging in discussion with an undocumented student; identifying an issue of personal bias and/or ignorance then intentionally placing themselves in the position to dialogue with a person from that group in order to engage that difference; and participating in deep reflection both in writing and through class discussions about controversial current issues.

When teaching a course of this nature, and as the semester goes on, many students become weary and are caught off guard by the all-consuming nature that comes along with learning this material. Sherry has customarily included a "fun and relaxation" day at the midpoint in the semester to help restore some energy to the group after engaging in such deep exploration about intense social matters. Given Lisa's background and role as a part of the instructor team, it seemed natural to bring together the "science" of leisure in the class discussion and demonstrate that fun is purposeful.

Fun is a conduit for positive emotions. The Broaden and Build Theory of Positive Emotions (Fredrickson, 2000) posits that positive emotions enhance psychological, intellectual, physical, and social resources. Johnson and Fredrickson (2005) conducted a study using facial recognition and the Broaden and Build Theory of Positive Emotions that has encouraging implications for multicultural education. Their results suggest that positive emotions, particularly joy, can possibly lessen some of the effects related to the negative perceptions associated with the social construction of race. A component of the Broaden and Build Theory is the "Undoing Effect" which postulates that positive emotions mitigate the damaging cardiovascular effects of negative emotions (Fredrickson, 2000).

Difficult dialogues in multicultural education are emotionally stressful. The body reacts to emotional stress in the same way it reacts to a physical threat (Sternberg, 2000). Stress is the physical and emotional response to a challenge (Sternberg, 2000). Stress accumulates and the body responds. The heart pumps blood toward the extremities and away from the heart and brain. The brain releases hormones that give the body the energy to fight or flee. The body and brain narrowly focus on a method of survival. Under stress, the body prepares to fight or flee and the mind focuses on a plan that has the best chance for individual survival. The stress associated with difficult dialogues can impede the outcome of diversity initiatives by narrowing a person's cognitive and physical response options. Positive emotions broaden response options, which can possibly alter how we view humanity and how we perceive systems that perpetuate oppression (Johnson and Fredrickson, 2005).

The goals of this unique classroom activity were to introduce students to the Broaden and Build Theory and to provide experiential opportunities for them to discover the physiological and emotional effects of positive emotions. The students entered the classroom with chairs arranged in a circle as a tangible way of embracing the Circle of Trust® practice. One instructor gave a brief overview of the class schedule and then played a short video about how the brain responds to positive and negative emotions. The video provided a scholarly introduction to the physiological benefits of positive emotions. After the video, the instructors led a ten-minute session of

Laughter Yoga. The purpose of Laughter Yoga was to give students the opportunity to disengage from "head" learning and engage in "heart and hand" learning. The class immersed themselves in the moment and fully participated. During the discussion following yoga, they shared that it made them feel lighter and more connected to the group.

The next activity was designed to allow students to experience their bodies within the context of various emotions. After the previous discussion, students were asked to take their pulse and write it down. Students were asked to chat with their partners about an enjoyable topic of their choice for five minutes, then take their pulse again and write it down. They noticed that their pulse had decreased. They were invited to continue their conversations. While they were engaged with each other, an instructor began a video with soothing music and students broke from conversation to watch it. The end of the video was scary, when it was over, students were told to immediately take their pulse again. They noticed that their pulse increased drastically. Students were encouraged to resume their pleasant conversations with their partners for several minutes then take their pulse again. They noticed that it decreased significantly. The discussion led to the importance of body awareness. They were able to experience how both positive and negative emotions had a significant physical impact on their hearts. As Parker Palmer (2011) states, "the heart is where everything begins" (p. 10). If the heart is a focal point of our work as multicultural educators, we need to find strategies that mend both the physical and the emotional aspects of the heart after we tax it. Students reflected on how to balance discomfort and positivity in their practice as higher education and student affairs professionals.

After a break, an audio commentary by Ben Mattlin (2010) was shared to bridge the Broaden and Build Theory to disability and ableism which was the topic being discussed at that point in the semester. Ben is a person born with a severe physical disability. He was admitted to Harvard in 1980, the year it was required to become accessible. He shared that he was not allowed to have a roommate because the dean did not want to "impair" the experience for able-bodied students. The dean gave no consideration to how this isolation would affect Ben's experience. In listening to this account of Ben's life, the students discussed the complexities of the institutional and psychological barriers that impeded the inclusion of persons with disabilities.

The final activity of the class that day was constructed to synthesize head, heart, and hand learning. Prior to this class, students were asked to reflect on and write down what they do for fun to reduce stress. Every student had included music as a means of stress management. The instructor team sent out an inquiry about the students' musical talents. One student responded that he was a singer; he agreed to lead the class in song. It was an amazing experience! The class sang with wild abandon outside the class building. Passersby listened and watched and professors came to their windows to enjoy the concert. When the second song ended and it was past the end of class, students lingered. They said they did not want it to be over, they laughed and talked and were much lighter than when they came to class.

It was lovely that the class period was enjoyable; the instructor team also wanted to know if the activities led to a greater understanding about positive emotions and their relationship to multicultural education and personal growth. Unsolicited, the day after that class, a student sent the instructor team an email, "It was a good mix of being 'real' and being silly, and I feel like we learned a lot about leisure in relation to stress and stress in relation to your place in society . . . I felt light and content for the rest of the afternoon, and I haven't really felt light for the past few months!"

Critical Reflections and Questions on Uses of Circles of Trust® with Multicultural Initiatives

While we had some wonderful success in leading this particular group, there have been times that other groups display being very uncomfortable with storytelling, poetry, and other forms of learning on the slant. These groups of students usually minimize these activities and label them as not "academic enough" and not "real learning." The irony is that no matter how careful the process is facilitated when you invite people to examine these long-held beliefs, even using the Circle of Trust® approach, resistance still rears its head and the group process can get off track.

Leading with the principles and practices of the Circle of Trust® approach can create a dynamic where accountability is situated differently than in other multicultural approaches. In subtle ways, the approach moves accountability for doing challenging work from the leaders to the participants. The Executive Director of the Center for Courage and Renewal, Terry Chadsey, retold a story about a man sharing with him that he felt like the Circle of Trust® work had been intense and he felt like the facilitators had "kicked his butt." Terry responded, "No, we held the space so you could kick your own butt" (personal communication, June 22, 2013). There are benefits to this approach and yet we are also left with some questions:

1. How might facilitators of multicultural education develop new ways to communicate important and classic messages about internalized oppression and internalized superiority (Potapchuk, Leiderman, Bivens, and Major, 2005)?

2. Is it possible to communicate these important and classic messages with softer approaches such as Circle of Trust® and still maintain the appropriate intensity? In other words, is the kinder and gentler way of engaging *Difference* such as within the Circle of Trust® approach and

making the association with positive emotions a reasonable solution to breaking down social oppression when the experience is neither kind nor gentle?

3. Can the combination of holding oneself accountable in the company of others have more of a lasting impact on one's skill development for engaging *Difference* than other forms of multicultural exploration?

These are a few questions we ponder as we continue to apply Courage work to multicultural initiatives.

Conclusions

In this course, students were able to strengthen their ability to engage with *Difference* through critical examination of inequitable policies and practices of institutions that help create and maintain the differential outcomes and stresses for marginalized groups (Potapchuk, Leiderman, Bivens, and Major, 2005). The Circle of Trust® approach provided a container where students could critically examine how they personally evolved within a society where race and other social oppressions have restricted the lives of both the marginalized and the dominant groups. How social oppression plays out has had a disproportionate impact on the education, employment, and social lives of marginalized groups within U.S. culture. Our instructor team tried to build within each student the stamina to engage *Difference* in order to address issues critical to the human race. If college educators continue to avoid placing intentional emphasis on developing the skills of college students to engage *Difference* productively, then our institutions may not be able to succeed in fully developing their students and the social problems of today will continue to be a struggle for equality that will hamper our ability to live as fully human.

References

Adams, M., Bell, L. A., and Griffin, P. *Teaching for Diversity and Social Justice.* 2nd ed. New York: Routledge Press, 2007.

Center for Courage & Renewal. *The Circle of Trust® Approach: Our Principles and Practices,* 2013. Retrieved July 7, 2013, from http://www.couragerenewal.org/about/foundations#principles

Chadsey, T., and Jackson, M. "Principles and Practices of the Circle of Trust® Approach." In M. Golden (ed.), *Teaching and Learning from the Inside Out: Revitalizing Ourselves and Our Institutions.* New Directions for Teaching and Learning, no. 130, 3–14. San Francisco: Jossey-Bass, 2012.

Fredrickson, B. L. "Cultivating Positive Emotions to Optimize Health and Well-Being." *Prevention Treatment,* 2000, 3. Retrieved from http://www.rickhanson.net/wp-content/files/papers/CultPosEmot.pdf

Golden, M. (ed.). *Teaching and Learning from the Inside Out: Revitalizing Ourselves and Our Institutions.* New Directions for Teaching and Learning, no. 130. San Francisco: Jossey-Bass, 2012.

hooks, b. *Teaching to Transgress: Education as the Practice of Freedom.* London: Routledge Press, 1994.

Johnson, K. J., and Fredrickson, B. L. "We All Look the Same to Me: Positive Emotions Eliminate the Own-Race Bias in Face Recognition." *Psychological Science*, 2005, *16*(11), 875–881. doi:10.1111/j.1467–9280.2005.01631.x

Mattlin, B. *Looking Back on 20 Years of Disability Rights*, 2010. Retrieved June 19, 2013, from http://www.npr.org/templates/story/story.php?storyId=128697147

Palmer, P. J. *Healing the Heart of Democracy: The Courage to Create a Politics Worthy of the Human Spirit.* Hoboken, N.J.: Jossey-Bass, 2011.

Pope, R. L., Reynolds, A. L., and Mueller, J. A. *Multicultural Competence in Student Affairs.* San Francisco: Jossey-Bass, 2004.

Potapchuk, M., Leiderman, S., Bivens, D., and Major, B. *Flipping the Script: White Privilege and Community Building.* Silver Springs, Md.: MP Associates, Inc., and the Center for Assessment and Policy Development (CAPD), 2005.

Sleeter, C. E., and Grant, C. A. *Making Choices for Multicultural Education: Five Approaches to Race, Class, and Gender.* 6th ed. San Francisco: John Wiley & Sons, Inc., 2008.

Sternberg, E. M. *The Balance Within: The Science Connecting Health and Emotions.* New York: W. H. Freeman, 2000.

Torres, V. "Using Student Development Theories to Explain Student Outcomes." In J. C. Smart (ed.), *Higher Education Handbook of Theory and Research XXVI.* Dordrecht: Springer, 2011.

SHERRY K. WATT *is an associate professor of higher education and student affairs at the University of Iowa. Her research on privileged identity exploration expands the understanding of the various ways in which people react to difficult dialogue.*

MARGARET GOLDEN *is a professor at Dominican University of California. She was prepared as a facilitator by the Center for Courage and Renewal.*

LISA A. P. SCHUMACHER *is the proprietor of Serenity Wellness Center and is a doctoral student at the University of Iowa.*

LUIS S. MORENO *is the dean of student services at Sauk Valley Community College and a doctoral candidate at the University of Iowa.*

7

The growing diversity and changing demographics within the United States increases the importance of students developing skills to engage across identity difference. The purpose of this chapter is to describe how a pre-employment course for student staff members is used as a multicultural intervention training to provide students with the knowledge and skills to create and facilitate an inclusive, multicultural community in residential communities.

Building Multicultural Residential Communities: A Model for Training Student Staff

Taryn Petryk, Monita C. Thompson, Trelawny Boynton

The growing diversity of the United States requires institutions of higher education to anticipate cultural differences from both a U.S. and a global context. The shifting demographics in the United States suggest that the population will be majority non-white by 2050 (U.S. Census Bureau, 2008). Gurin, Nagda, and Zúñiga (2013) suggest that increases in enrollment of Hispanic, African American, and Asian students, while white student enrollment decreases, create an important trend in higher education. In addition, immigration will provide a significant increase in the population of college students (Murdock and Hoque, 1999; Passel and Cohn, 2008). These likely demographic changes will provide a dynamic environment for learning as well as a challenge to higher education institutions to create communities of inclusivity and respect for differences.

Moving into a new environment, away from daily interactions and influences of family and former peers, provides students with new opportunities to learn and develop (Blimling and Miltenberger, 1995). Residential communities (residence halls and apartments) provide a multicultural living environment where students interact and live with individuals from varying cultures and social identity groups, which are often different from their home environment. Residential student staffs are charged with creating multicultural living environments inclusive of all residents and are often the first institutional representatives new students meet. This initial contact sets the tone and climate for helping students navigate the social and academic environments of their institution. For example, residents use

New Directions for Student Services, no. 144, Winter 2013 © 2013 Wiley Periodicals, Inc.
Published online in Wiley Online Library (wileyonlinelibrary.com) • DOI: 10.1002/ss.20070

the community kitchens to cook foods that represent their cultures; the aromas while cooking challenge students to reconsider what smells "good" and "bad" and that sometimes these perceptions are based on their frame of reference and understanding of other cultures. If a conflict arises around kitchen use, it is situations like these require that student staff intervene to help students negotiate across difference.

At the University of Michigan, University Housing Residence Education has developed an academic course required for all student residential staff (Diversity Peer Educators, Resident Advisors, and Peer Academic Success Specialists) to prepare them for their respective jobs. Although each of the positions has unique responsibilities, their common goal is to provide a safe and supportive environment for every student in the residence community. The course, Social Psychology in Community Settings, serves as intervention training to provide students with the knowledge for being effective staff members. It also incorporates development of the skills one needs to live and work in our global society. Gurin (2013) suggests the skills that are needed for the twenty-first century are communication, problem solving, collaboration across difference, critical and flexible thinking, empathy, as well as the ability to nurture a pluralistic perspective. The course focuses on community building from a multicultural perspective.

Many of our students come from diverse backgrounds yet often have not encountered others who have different experiences from their own based on social identity. The presence of diversity in the student population creates an opportunity to engage students in learning about others as well as themselves while in order to better understand the value of difference. This course provides opportunities for students to engage in these learning experiences as participants and practice facilitating these experiences for their residents.

Course Development

Considering the various issues that affect an inclusive and supportive environment in residential communities, the course was developed as an intentional collaboration between Residence Education, The Program on Intergroup Relations, and a faculty member. Each brings a particular strength to the design of the program areas.

Residence Education provides practical knowledge about the living environment and opportunity for "real" experiential learning. Furthermore, the trained program staff members who lead the course understand how to build inclusive residential communities with students from differing backgrounds and developmental levels (Piper and Buckley, 2004). The second partner, the Program on Intergroup Relations (IGR), is a nationally recognized program for developing intergroup dialogues in higher education. As the first such program in higher education, it is well known specifically for its work with training peer facilitators in intergroup dialogue and social justice education. IGR brings a wealth of experience with pedagogy that uses cognitive and experiential learning methods, as well as dialogic techniques to provide a classroom environment that integrates learning from students lived experience and course materials. The faculty member is the third partner to the course and provides the academic connection. Social inequality, intergroup interactions, and building interpersonal empathy are important aspects of the course that draw upon the rich social psychology literature that relates to students' work across identities and in inclusive communities (Dovidio and Gaertner, 2004; Stephan and Finlay, 1999). The faculty member's participation connects the course academic credit for students and this serves as validation of the importance of the educational value of the residential student work.

The faculty member and one representative from each area serve as lead coordinators for the course. These coordinators develop the curriculum, select and train small group facilitators, provide leadership throughout the semester, and oversee course assessment.

Structure and Co-Facilitation

Although the course is constructed to engage students in integrated learning and reflection, the large number of students (180–200 each year) all together prohibits the type of exploration necessary for deep learning to occur. Instead, the course is divided into small groups of 12–16 students and is co-facilitated by an experienced student and a professional staff member. The goal is to select a diverse team of professional and student staff that encompass a variety of experiences and social identities. The benefits of having a diverse team of co-facilitations for the small groups are that each brings their own complementary styles; there is a mix of social identities as well as professional and student roles. As with the intergroup dialogue model, it is important for course participants to have access to someone who has a social identity similar to their own, specifically a facilitator who has knowledge of privilege, power, and difference and can empathize with the learning edges that arise when talking about these issues (Zúñiga, Nagda, Chesler, and Cytron-Walker, 2007).

Curriculum

Using theory, practice, and experiential learning, the course engages students personally and encourages them to draw upon their own knowledge and experiences as part of the learning process. Influenced by the four-stage intergroup dialogue model (Zúñiga, Nagda, Chesler, and Cytron-Walker, 2007), the course has four modules integrated over eleven weeks: identity development, power and privilege in intergroup relations, working through conflict, and communication and ally development. The focus is based on understanding and bridging identity differences and is explicitly geared toward putting those concepts into action when serving as a staff member in a residence community setting. The course meets fourteen times, with an introductory session for the entire large group, twelve small group sessions, and a culminating event. The curriculum is designed to elaborate on each module through utilizing journals, readings, media, assignments, and experiential activities to emphasize the partnership between academic and student services.

Identity Development.   Identity exploration is the basis for students to begin to understand their own and others' gender, sexual orientation, race, ethnicity, religious/faith affiliation, ability status, and other social identities. It is the foundation for all other learning in our curriculum. Residence staff must first gain an understanding of who they are and the types of experiences that have an effect on how they view themselves and others. While identity development can (and does) occur throughout the life cycle, college students are formulating who they are, independent of family, friends, influential people, and social structures, which have thus far provided information and guidance to them. Baxter Magolda (2001) describes this part of a students' journey as the first phase of self-authorship, "The Crossroads," where students begin the search for internally defining their beliefs, goals, values, and self-definition. The readings that provide a foundation for this module include Beverly Tatum's (1997) "The Complexity of Identity: Who Am I?" as well as various first person narratives on social identity exploration. Activities that provide an experiential bridge in this module may include the Social Identity Profile where students are asked to identify the group memberships to which they belong and to reflect on how these identities will affect their interactions in the residential communities. For example, students are asked to consider how their race and/or ethnicity will impact on how they enter conflict mediation with individuals who are different from themselves. Students also develop and share a "testimonial" on two of their salient identities as a way of deeply exploring the understanding of their own socialization. Sharing their own stories, listening to others, and connecting these personal stories to group identities better prepare residence staff to empathize with others and understand the important role that social identities play in building inclusive communities.

Power and Privilege in Intergroup Relations.   The second module is developed to help students examine personal values, biases, and attitudes that they hold about race, gender, class, ethnicity, religion, age, sexual orientation, disability, and other identities. Students learn to recognize how these values and attitudes influence their decision making, particularly in regard to building community, creating resident programs, and supporting students individually. The primary goal is to analyze difference, privilege, justice, and injustice as they apply to a residential setting. The learning that occurs in the second module helps staff to understand how these issues come into play when mediating conflicts, confronting behaviors, and planning community builder programs. The "Social Inequality on Campus" group assignment is an example of how this type of learning is facilitated. Students work in small groups to explore a social inequality on campus and its effects on students and the dynamics of the community. Readings that support this type of active learning include chapters from Allen Johnson's (2006) book, *Privilege, Power, and Difference,* as well as additional readings that showcase personal experiences around discrimination and oppression. This assignment allows students to think critically about inequalities that exist within their own communities and brings to life the classroom conversations, readings, and assignments. Students are able to reflect on their sphere of influence to act on inequalities that may exist in their residential communities.

Working through Conflict and Communication.   Managing conflict and communication effectively with all residents is an important job responsibility for student staff. The vast majority of conflict involves issues related to culture, social identity, beliefs, and values. Successful conflict resolution is often determined by the skill level of the staff managing these situations and encouraging individuals to talk about the underlying issues of the conflict (Blimling, 1993). Many conflict resolution situations often stem from disagreements as a result of residence-hall-related policy infractions, roommate differences, and community living standards. This module focuses on understanding personal conflict and communication styles within the context of residential communities.

One way that students are able to explore the above is through an activity called the "Listening Exercise." This exercise is used to deepen active listening skills while exploring the ways in which the students own family units handled emotions as conflict when growing up. In triads, the students explore a conflict (the how, what, and when of issues). Each student has the opportunity to be a listener and an observer while the talker addresses questions that refer to the above topics. Through reflection, peer feedback, and large group debriefing, students gain insight into how their past experiences affect how they will respond when conflict, emotions, and differing forms of communication styles are present in the residence hall. The students also read Janet Rifkin and Leah Wing's (2001) chapter "Racial Identity Development and the Readings/Videotion of Conflicts" from Jackson and Wijeyesinghe's book, *New Perspectives on Racial Identity Development: A Theoretical and Practical Anthology.*

The culminating event, "Behind Community Doors," occurs at the end of the semester and allows students to practice responding to relevant situations involving social identity within the residential environment.

Ally Development.   This last module bridges the learning of the first three modules that focus specifically on developing intrapersonal and interpersonal awareness and skills by exploring what it means to be an ally and to assess the role of an ally as it relates to building an inclusive community.

New Directions for Student Services • DOI: 10.1002/ss

Residential staff are asked to create and sustain an environment where all social identities feel safe and welcomed in their community. This is a challenging component of the position. It is important for staff to identify both their areas of intergroup strength and knowledge and those they need to develop.

In addition to readings on social justice ally development, such as Keith Edwards's (2006) article, "Aspiring Social Justice Ally Identity Development," students are asked to fill out an ally profile that guides reflection on their own awareness, skills, knowledge, and abilities to take ally action on all social identities. Through small group conversations, this activity allows individuals to see areas for growth and support.

Assessment and Evaluation.   Throughout the semester, students develop an ePortfolio (electronic portfolio) to demonstrate to their facilitators and future supervisors in the residential communities what they have learned about identity, inequality, conflict, and ally development, and what skills they have gained that will make them an effective staff member. Zubizarreta (2009) states, "The learning portfolio is a rich, convincing, and adaptable method of recording intellectual growth and involving students in a critically reflective, collaborative process" (p. xxvii). The ePortfolio provides a representation of their integrated learning and skill development that they can refer back to as well as change and amplify as they function in their residence staff and other organizational/community roles.

Students also have an opportunity to provide feedback around course curriculum and co-facilitators through the course evaluations provided by the Office of the Registrar. To ensure that the goals and learning outcomes are being met, we utilize these evaluations as well as feedback from the facilitators on the curriculum to adapt and modify the course on a yearly basis.

Course Challenges

Four major areas have been identified as crucial to the development of residential staff in building inclusive communities: understanding multiple identities and intersectionality, contradictions between personal values and employment expectations, understanding underlying issues of conflict, and application to the staff position. This section will explore how these areas create challenges that arise with implementing the course and how we address them.

Understanding Multiple Identities and Intersectionality.   Time is spent in the course identifying social-group memberships and how social identities are impacted by privilege and oppression in society. As these concepts are explored, students experience difficulty connecting multiple identities and understanding the concept of intersectionality. There are times when privileged and oppressed identities cannot be separated and

NEW DIRECTIONS FOR STUDENT SERVICES • DOI: 10.1002/ss

students often default to focusing on their marginalized identities rather than those where advantages are awarded. As mentioned earlier in this chapter, testimonials are introduced to assist students in keeping a perspective that includes all of their identities. Testimonials also provide facilitators with insights as to where students are in their understanding of privilege so they can assist students through their journey.

Contradictions between Personal Values and Employment Expectations. Throughout the course, students begin to discover contradictions between their beliefs, values, and expectations of the course. One of the goals of the course is for students to understand and develop ally behaviors to use in their staff positions. Broido (2000) describes social justice allies as members of dominant social groups who are working to end the system of oppression that gives them greater privilege and power based on their social-group membership. In the context of their role, student staff need to be aware of the ways in which residents' social identities are impacted by privilege and oppression, and actively work to create environments where students of all identities are supported. Conflict arises when students' beliefs and values target another social group. One way we have observed this conflict manifest is in a student whose religious identity holds beliefs that oppress lesbian, gay, bisexual, and transgender students. Here, oppression may range from discomfort in discussing LGBTQ experiences to outright refusal to support residents. Determining and communicating clear expectations of staff members around ally behavior is important and crucial to the mission, vision, and values of the Housing organization. In these conversations, facilitators relay to students that if they are unable to meet these expectations of an ally, then the staff position may not be for them. The course coordinators consider this expectation when making staff position decisions.

Understanding Underlying Issues of Conflict. Given the course consists of personal experiences and narratives of power and privilege, conflicting opinions and perceptions will emerge. Students perceive conflict in different ways, and their attitudes on conflict are often negative. Further, students see conflict as oppositional and argument-debate based. Working through conflict and understanding the underlying issues on interpersonal, intergroup, and cultural levels is a hurdle for many students. Facilitators reframe dialogue as a method for students to work through differences and conflict. They also assist students in naming and exploring how identity and culture shape our conflict attitudes and behaviors. The hope is that students leave the course with experiences that demonstrate how conflict can be a necessary part of the learning process and how social identity impacts situations in residential communities.

Application to the Staff Position. The last challenge is one that persists as the course evolves over the semester. It presents a simple question: how do students take what they have learned and put it to use in the residence hall and apartment communities? This is particularly challenging as we cover such a volume of material, exercises, and concepts. It is critical for facilitators to link the theories explored in the group settings to how they will build community in their residence halls. We attempt to mediate this challenge and make the connection to their day-to-day work by asking reflective questions, linking experiences to their own community settings, and encouraging them to utilize the information gathered in their ePortfolio as a guide for their work. In addition, we acknowledge that more work must be done after the course to ensure that supervisors within the communities reinforce the course content throughout the year with their residential staff as they are leading their residents.

Application for Other Campuses

First and foremost, the commitment of the course requires support from all levels of the institution. It is important that commitment is supported through clearly communicated mission and vision statements that indicate the department's stance on identity, inclusion, and social justice. At the University of Michigan, these declarations exist at multiple levels in the Division of Student Affairs, Housing's Living at Michigan credo, and values of Residence Education.

Inclusive hiring practices must exist if a unit decides to engage in socially just work. In order to have a representative staff across the social spectrum, supervisors have to understand the value of difference. Therefore, supervisors must be trained in order to equip them with the skills to work within diverse teams. They need to develop these tools by having training experiences that is similar to what the students received via the course. To assist in consistency across the department, all Residence Education professional staff attend an annual two-day workshop that is focused on exploring concepts of identity, privilege, oppression, and ally work.

We considered the concentration structure for the course, both for student participants and facilitators. By offering course credit to students (both as participants and as facilitators), it is rendered significant because it exists both in the academic and co-curricular realms. Students are held accountable both academically and as a condition for employment. Facilitating this course adds an additional 8–10 hours of work per week for the duration of the course. It is critical to explore ways to recognize the significant contributions of facilitators. As mentioned above, student facilitators are offered three academic credits for taking on this role. Financial compensation is given to both student and professional staff facilitators (though course coordinators are not compensated). Given the ever-changing fiscal climate, this may not be a sustainable model for other campuses. Regardless, it is critical to explore ways to recognize the significant contributions of facilitators.

NEW DIRECTIONS FOR STUDENT SERVICES • DOI: 10.1002/ss

The course outlined is only one component of building an inclusive multicultural residential community at the University of Michigan. Given the changing demographics and the ever-evolving nature of campus communities, our staff has ongoing training that considers social justice aspects of the environment. It is important that we remain attuned to demographic changes and that we are constantly exploring ways to support all students in the community. This course is a useful tool and will be updated as needed to reflect the needs of the students who attend our university and the changes in the residential community environment.

References

Baxter Magolda, M. B. *Making Town Way: Narratives for Transforming Higher Education to Promote Self-Authorship.* Sterling, Va.: Stylus, 2001.

Blimling, G. S. (ed.). *The Experienced Resident Assistant: Readings, Case Studies and Structured Group Exercises for Advanced Training.* 2nd ed. Dubuque, Iowa: Kendall/Hunt Publishing, 1993.

Blimling, G. S., and Miltenberger, L. K. *The Resident Assistant: Working with College Students in Residence Halls.* Dubuque, Iowa: Kendall/Hunt Publishing Company, 1995.

Broido, E. M. "The Development of Social Justice Allies During College: A Phenomenological Investigation." *Journal of College Student Development,* 2000, *41,* 3–17.

Dovidio, J. F., and Gaertner, S. L. "Aversive Racism." *Advances in Experimental Social Psychology,* 2004, *36,* 1–52.

Edwards, K. "Aspiring Social Justice Ally Identity Development: A Conceptual Model." *NASPA Journal,* 2006, *43*(4), 39–60.

Gurin, P. *Engaging Diversity: It's Importance for 21st Century Education.* Speech, Ann Arbor, Mich., February 27, 2013.

Gurin, P., Nagda, B. A., and Zúñiga, X. *Dialogue Across Difference: Practice, Theory and Research on Intergroup Dialogue.* New York: Russell Sage Foundation, 2013.

Johnson, A. *Privilege, Power, and Difference.* New York: McGraw-Hill, 2006.

Murdock, S. H., and Hoque, M. N. "Demographic Factors Affecting Higher Education in the United States in the Twenty-First Century." In G. H. Gaither (ed.), *Promising Practices in Recruitment, Remediation, and Retention.* New Directions for Higher Education, no. 108, 5–13. San Francisco: Jossey-Bass, 1999.

Passel, J. S., and Cohn, D. V. *U.S. Population Projections: 2005–2050,* 2008. Washington, DC: Pew Research Center. Retrieved January 27, 2013, from http://pewhispanic.org/files/reports/85.pdf

Piper, T. D., and Buckley, J. A. "Community Standards Model: Developing Learning Partnerships in Campus Housing." In M. Baxter Magolda and P. M. King (eds.), *Learning Partnerships: Theory and Models of Practice to Educate for Self-Authorship.* Sterling, Va.: Stylus, 2004.

Rifkin, J., and Wing, L. "Racial Identity Development and the Readings/Videotion of Conflicts." In B. Jackson and C. Wijeyesinghe (eds.), *New Perspectives on Racial Identity Development: A Theoretical and Practical Anthology.* New York: New York University Press, 2001.

Stephan, W. G., and Finlay, K. "The Role of Empathy in Improving Intergroup Relations." *Journal of Social Issues,* 1999, *55*(4), 729–743.

Tatum, B. "The Complexity of Identity: Who Am I?" *Why Are All The Black Kids Sitting Together in the Cafeteria?* New York: Basic Books, Perseus Book Group, 1997.

U.S. Census Bureau. *An Older and More Diverse Nation by Midcentury*. Washington, D.C.: Government Printing Office, 2008.

Zubizarreta, J. *The Learning Portfolio: Reflective Practice for Improving Student Learning*. San Francisco: Jossey-Bass, 2009.

Zúñiga, X., Nagda, B. A., Chesler, M., and Cytron-Walker, A. "Intergroup Dialogue in Higher Education: Meaningful Learning about Social Justice." *ASHE Higher Education Report*, 32(4). San Francisco: Jossey-Bass, 2007.

TARYN PETRYK *is the director of co-curricular programs, The Program on Intergroup Relations, The University of Michigan.*

MONITA C. THOMPSON *is the assistant dean of students and co-director, The Program on Intergroup Relations, The University of Michigan.*

TRELAWNY BOYNTON *is the director of diversity and inclusion for University Housing, The University of Michigan.*

NEW DIRECTIONS FOR STUDENT SERVICES • DOI: 10.1002/ss

8

This chapter reviews the impact of using race caucuses with members of a student affairs leadership team to deepen their capacity to both recognize common dynamics of racism, internalized dominance, and internalized oppression, and explore specific strategies to create greater equity in their organization.

Race Caucuses: An Intensive, High-Impact Strategy to Create Social Change

Kathy Obear, becky martinez

Race caucuses can be a powerful multicultural initiative to deepen the competencies of higher education administrators and student affairs practitioners to create equitable, inclusive campus environments for students and staff. The purpose of this chapter is to discuss the outcomes from using race caucuses at a large public university and offer a critique of this methodology as a tool for professional development.

Most higher education administrators and student affairs practitioners have participated in some form of diversity training, and yet many have not developed the critical competencies necessary to dismantle institutional racism. Too often multicultural initiatives are narrowly focused solely on "valuing diversity" and discussing the experiences of members of marginalized groups. This "diversity as good" approach (Watt, 2011, p. 131) falls into one or more of the following pitfalls: increasing staff self-awareness about issues of race and racism without significant skill development to create racially equitable and inclusive programs, policies, and services; focusing on increasing knowledge without a parallel emphasis on affective elements crucial to unlearning racism and developing staff as change agents; and locating the responsibility for organizational change with staff of color without an intentional strategy to develop whites as allies in creating inclusive campus environments.

It is imperative that college administrators deepen their capacity to recognize and dismantle policies, practices, and services that, often unintentionally, disproportionately advantage whites and disadvantage people of color. Broido (2000) argues that ally work encompasses three components: educating members of privileged groups, creating organization and cultural change, and supporting members of marginalized groups. Race caucuses provide a forum for the development of skills in these three areas as well as

New Directions for Student Services, no. 144, Winter 2013 © 2013 Wiley Periodicals, Inc.
Published online in Wiley Online Library (wileyonlinelibrary.com) • DOI: 10.1002/ss.20071

a space to engage in authentic dialogue and personal work critical to developing capacity to create sustainable organizational change that eliminates racial barriers to student success.

Race Caucuses

Identity group caucuses are a common learning methodology used in Social Justice Education and Intergroup Dialogue (Adams, Bell, and Griffin, 2007; Wijeyesinghe, Griffin, and Love, 1997; Zúñiga, Nagda, and Sevig, 2002). Homogeneous caucus groups provide participants a more intimate, supportive, and comfortable space to stimulate honest self-reflection and explore various ways that race, racism, internalized dominance, and internalized oppression impact their lives (Abdullah and McCormack, 2008; Walls and others, 2009; Wijeyesinghe, Griffin, and Love, 1997). This methodology can help participants discuss common issues, themes, and concerns (Adams, 2007) that they may be hesitant to initially raise in a cross-race setting (Griffin and Harro, 1997; Walls and others, 2009; Wijeyesinghe, Griffin, and Love, 1997).

Caucuses can enhance meaningful dialogue about controversial topics and provide opportunity to discuss more intimate issues and experiences before sharing them in the larger group (Abdullah and McCormack, 2008; Zúñiga, Nagda, and Sevig, 2002). Facilitators contribute significantly to the learning process as they authentically share their own struggles and feelings, recognize times they experience white privilege, and acknowledge examples of their racist attitudes and behaviors or collusion (Walls and others, 2009).

Participants choose to attend the race caucus that most aligns with their racial identity. The white caucus is for people who identify as white and/or who experience white skin privilege, including those who are bi/multiracial with white ancestry. The people of color caucus is for those who identify as Latino/a, black or African American, API (Asian/Asian America/Pacific Islander), Native American or Indigenous, Middle Eastern/Arab, and Bi/Multiracial. Facilitators need to hold the same racial identity of the caucus they lead (Griffin and Harro, 1997).

People of color often express relief when able to gather and talk openly about racism, internalized oppression, and collusion without potential resistance and defensiveness from white participants (Wijeyesinghe, Griffin, and Love, 1997). While this space is often unfamiliar for many people of color, they are able to connect and support each other through dynamics resulting from racism. During this time, horizontal hostility may arise providing the opportunity for authentic dialogue across targeted racial groups. As people of color explore their own internalized oppression, they are able to dismantle stereotypes they may hold about their racial group(s), other targeted racial groups, and whites. In doing so, they are able to discover and confront racist dynamics on the individual, group, and systems level (martinez, 2010; Wijeyesinghe, Griffin, and Love, 1997). People of color are also able to explore ways they have colluded with racist dynamics and what they need in order to heal and liberate themselves from racism.

The goal of a white caucus is to help participants develop competencies, attitudes, and courage to effectively engage issues of race and racism on campus. Key learning outcomes include the ability to recognize whiteness, white privilege, and internalized dominance, and to acknowledge feelings of guilt, shame, defensiveness, and embarrassment in order to shift these emotions into passion and commitment to create meaningful change in themselves and their environment (Wijeyesinghe, Griffin, and Love, 1997). In sharp contrast to the sense of relief that many participants of color experience in caucuses, whites are often reluctant to engage in caucuses and doubt that any meaningful learning can occur without the presence of people of color (Wijeyesinghe, Griffin, and Love, 1997). Some may resist out of concern that the structure creates further separation and division among whites and people of color (Griffin and Harro, 1997).

A key benefit of white caucuses is that whites often realize the damage they have experienced from the impact of racism in their lives, including building their sense of self on the illusion that whites are superior to people of color; believing that they have earned their place in society solely from their own competence and hard work; acting in ways that violate their core values by treating people of color based on racist attitudes and stereotypes; living in isolation without any authentic connections with people of color; coping with deep feelings of guilt, fear, shame, and inadequacy; and losing real intimacy and community with white allies (Kivel, 1996). Another benefit is that whites realize that they can learn from each other and take responsibility for dismantling racism without subjecting people of color to any further pain or discomfort as we openly discuss our racist attitudes and behaviors (Abdullah and McCormack, 2008).

It is common practice in both Intergroup Dialogue and Social Justice Education to facilitate a conversation in a full cross-race group after caucus sessions to discuss and share common themes, the impact of learning in same-racial group caucuses, and strategies to create community and liberation. It can be powerful for whites to hear more directly about the day-to-day impact of racism from their colleagues of color as well as for people of color to hear whites acknowledge the privilege and internalized dominance they experience and take responsibility for creating change in themselves and the work environment (Wijeyesinghe, Griffin, and Love, 1997).

Race Caucuses as a Multicultural Initiative

In the following sections, we outline the central elements of the multicultural initiative we facilitated using race caucuses for higher education administrators at a large, public university. We received a request for a training session to help the top thirty student affairs leaders and directors increase their capacity to engage in authentic dialogue and strategic change efforts that address dynamics of race and racism on campus and within the division of student affairs. After talking with the top leaders of the division, we chose to use race caucuses because the leaders could discuss racial issues at a conceptual level, but most did not demonstrate the ability to talk honestly about their own experiences as raced beings nor acknowledge or respond to racial dynamics that occurred in discussions and meetings. We believed that exploring issues of internalized dominance and internalized racism in race caucuses would provide participants the opportunity to develop competence, compassion, and courage necessary for creating sustainable racial equity on campus.

We designed a 1.5-day event and planned for the race caucuses to occur on day 1 and for the full group to engage in cross-race dialogue on the morning of the next day. Key activities during the people of color caucus included the opportunity for participants to connect and form community with other people of color. They discussed their struggles on campus with race and racist dynamics, including those with other targeted racial groups. Through storytelling they were able to validate and normalize their lived experience and the resulting internalized oppression, which impacted their emotional, physical, and mental health. Participants discussed their needs with each other to deal with and dismantle racism while healing and liberating themselves from racist dynamics. Lastly, in this newly empowered space, participants developed strategies to work with their white colleagues in authentic, meaningful ways.

Because people of color were rarely afforded the opportunity to spend time together as a group, it took them time to not focus the discussion on their white colleagues and what they needed from them. After reflecting on their behavior and some guiding questions, they were able to shift the dialogue to their individual and collective experiences. Participants discussed the desire to connect with each other but struggled to do so because of lack of time and not knowing how to do so without their white colleagues questioning them. In addition, they realized that they did not know how to engage and be authentic with each other as a result of whiteness. This element of the design was the most critical for the group to connect and support each other. At this point, they were able to authentically share their stories, which included their struggles, pain, and challenges with other people of color and whites. In working through some of their internalized oppression, participants became clear on their needs and ways to ask for them from other colleagues of color as well as their white colleagues.

Key activities during the white caucus included the opportunity for participants to discuss their commitment to dismantle racism and create racial equity as well as their feelings about participating in a white caucus. They explored examples of progress as well as common microaggressions toward people of color, such as dismissing their frustrations as

NEW DIRECTIONS FOR STUDENT SERVICES • DOI: 10.1002/ss

overreactions, undervaluing their contributions, and constantly questioning the accuracy and legitimacy of statements from people of color. A critical section involved authentically describing times participants believed that whites were superior to people of color as well as common racist behaviors and attitudes that perpetuate and maintain unproductive team dynamics and institutional racism. Participants then discussed specific behaviors and strategies to interrupt racism and the benefits of creating greater equity and inclusion in both interpersonal dynamics and organizational practices (Goodman, 2011; Kivel, 1996).

Possibly the most critical element in this design involved the participants acknowledging times they had each reacted based on racist attitudes and behaviors or sought personal advantage by using white privilege. There was a sense of relief and freedom from honestly claiming their racist behaviors and realizing "I am not alone" and that their colleagues struggled with a similar depth of internalized dominance. The participants reported an increased ability to recognize racist attitudes and behaviors in the moment and a greater willingness to interrupt these dynamics in themselves and others. In addition, several participants expressed a strong desire to no longer act in ways that undermined their collaboration with other white allies, including competing with other whites to be seen as "the good one," distancing themselves from other whites by judging their behaviors and attitudes without relating in and owning how they have similar reactions, and moving away from talking about race by focusing on other areas of oppression where they have marginalized identities.

We designed the full cross-race group dialogue on the morning of the second day to provide participants the opportunity to engage in authentic conversations about both their experiences and insights from their race caucus as well as current dynamics of race and racism in the division and on campus. In addition, the leaders discussed strategies to create greater racial equity and negotiated specific action steps to continue their learning, the depth of authentic dialogue, and organizational change.

Outcomes

Participants identified several key outcomes as they reflected on the impact of the race caucuses and cross-race dialogue, including an increase in their ability to engage in authentic dialogue about race across racial identities; greater capacity to recognize dynamics of internalized dominance and internalized racism in daily interactions and practices; a deeper understanding of how dynamics of race and racism impact colleagues and students; an appreciation for the commitment of colleagues across race to create racial equity and inclusion on campus; and increased willingness to continue this level of dialogue both in leadership meetings and daily activities with colleagues and students.

Lessons Learned

While many participants expressed appreciation for their learning and insights from the race caucuses, on reflection, the outcomes could have been greatly enhanced by the following changes.

Position Race Caucuses within a Larger Organizational Culture Change Effort. The impact of using race caucuses as a multicultural initiative will be far greater if the experience is situated within a comprehensive organizational change effort. Instead of viewing the caucus experience as a stand-alone event, participants would realize that they are expected to transfer their insights and skills into daily practice as they infuse issues of racial equity and inclusion into policies, practices, services, and programs.

Ensure All Participants Have a Common Foundation of Inclusion Awareness and Skills Training about the Full Breadth of Privileged and Marginalized Group Dynamics on Campus. In our experience, participants in race caucuses, especially whites, are more willing to explore issues of privilege and internalized dominance/racism after they have had the opportunity in facilitated workshops to discuss and explore their multiple, intersecting marginalized and privileged group memberships. In addition, people of color and people who are bi/multiracial are more willing to engage in authentic dialogue with whites after they have been given space to explore their privilege and advantage in other areas of difference as well as share their own experiences of marginalization.

Provide Learning Opportunities for Participants to Develop a Shared Understanding of a Common Set of Concepts and Terms. It may be useful to establish prerequisites for participating in race caucuses, including assigned pre-readings and/or attendance at a foundational workshop on race and racism, so that participants share a common understanding of basic concepts.

Establish a Framework of Accountability. There are a number of accountability structures that could increase the likelihood of learning application and systemic change, including creating performance expectations and establishing clear performance indicators for all staff; requiring pre- and post-meetings between participants and their supervisor to review expectations and identify development goals for performance management processes; and conducting quarterly meetings with their supervisor to assess progress toward performance goals. These accountability structures assume that supervisors demonstrate the multicultural competencies and capacity to support the professional development of staff.

Provide Follow-Up Training Sessions Every Four to Six Months to Deepen Development of Cultural Competencies. Recommended topics for ongoing professional development include the following: review current data (quantitative and qualitative) about the racial climate on campus and in the division; identify policies, programs, services, and practices that (may unintentionally) create racial inequity in the division and discuss ways to shift those to create equity and inclusion; explore examples of racist behaviors and attitudes still tracked within the division; identify examples of white ally behaviors and efforts by people of color in the division to interrupt racist behaviors and practices; share organizational change practices implemented in units across the division; develop tools and strategies to navigate triggering events; and discuss where people still "feel stuck" and identify strategies for creating greater inclusion and racial equity.

Conduct Required Professional Development Activities That Explore Other Areas of Oppression.   Develop and implement a professional development plan that addresses inequity related to a full range of intersecting issues including sex; gender identity and expression; socio-economic class; ability and accessibility; sexual orientation; religion, belief, and spirituality; national origin and immigration status; and hierarchical dynamics related to job function, department, and position within the division.

Suggestions for Using Race Caucuses in Different Settings

There are some predictable challenges for implementing race caucuses on some campuses. Three are discussed here.

Demographics.   Many divisions of student affairs do not have enough leaders and managers of color to conduct caucuses within the division. A minimum number of participants is six to eight people. It may be possible to broaden the potential participants to include staff of color from throughout the division or colleagues of color from other administrative and faculty units.

Size of Leadership Team.   On smaller campuses the number of leaders and managers may be too small. Another approach is to invite colleagues from local colleges and universities to participate in regional race caucuses or to include all of the members of the student affairs division in the process.

Access to Skilled Facilitators.   Many campuses may not have staff or faculty who demonstrate the full breadth of critical facilitation competencies to lead race caucuses. Facilitators need the ability to create a container for deep authentic dialogue, self-disclosure, and personal storytelling (martinez, 2010) and the capacity to use triggering events as teachable moments (Obear, 2013). In addition, facilitators need to effectively engage resistance and defensiveness from members of privileged (Watt, 2007) and marginalized groups. It may be possible to use skilled facilitators from the local region or external consultants.

Closing Thoughts

Race-alike caucuses provide participants the opportunity to deepen their capacity to recognize the common dynamics of racism, internalized dominance and internalized oppression, explore specific strategies to create greater equity in their organizations, and develop the courage to step up as change agents. Participating in caucuses can develop effective relationships

NEW DIRECTIONS FOR STUDENT SERVICES • DOI: 10.1002/ss

within and across racial groups for future partnership and collaboration in creating inclusive campus environments and racial equity for all.

References

Abdullah, C. M., and McCormack, S. *Dialogue for Affinity Groups: Optional Discussions to Accompany Facing Racism in a Diverse Nation,* 2008. Retrieved February 5, 2013, from http://www.everyday-democracy.org/en/Resource.95.aspx

Adams, M. "Pedagogical Frameworks for Social Justice Education." In M. Adams, L. A. Bell, and P. Griffin, (eds.), *Teaching for Diversity and Social Justice.* 2nd ed. New York: Routledge, 2007.

Adams, M., Bell, L. A., and Griffin, P. (eds.), *Teaching for Diversity and Social Justice.* 2nd ed. New York: Routledge, 2007.

Broido, E. M. "Ways of Being an Ally to Lesbian, Gay, and Bisexual Students." In V. A. Wall and N. J. Adams (eds.), *Toward Acceptance: Sexual Orientation Issues on Campus.* Lanham, Md.: University Press of America, 2000.

Goodman, D. J. *Promoting Diversity and Social Justice: Educating People from Privileged Groups.* 2nd ed. New York: Routledge, 2011.

Griffin, P., and Harro, B. "Heterosexism Curriculum Design." In M. Adams, L. A. Bell, and P. Griffin (eds.), *Teaching for Diversity and Social Justice.* New York: Routledge, 1997.

Kivel, P. *Uprooting Racism: How White People Can Work for Racial Justice.* Gabriola Island, B.C., Canada: New Society Publishers, 1996.

martinez, b. "Linking Transformative Learning and Social Justice Through the Lens of Racism." Unpublished doctoral dissertation, Organizational Leadership Department, University of La Verne, 2010.

Obear, K. "Navigating Triggering Events: Critical Competencies for Social Justice Educators." In L. M. Landreman (ed.), *The Art of Effective Facilitation: Reflections from Social Justice Educators.* Sterling, Va.: Stylus, 2013.

Walls, N. E., Griffin, R., Arnold-Renicker, H., Burson, M., Johnston, C., Moorman, N., Nelsen, J., and Schutte, E. C. "Mapping Graduate Social Work Student Learning Journeys about Heterosexual Privilege." *Journal of Social Work Education,* 2009, 45(2), 289–307.

Watt, S. K. "Developing Cultural Competence: Facilitating Privileged Identity Exploration in Student Affairs Practice." *College Student Affairs Journal 2007 Special Issue,* 2007, 26(2), 114–126.

Watt, S. K. "Moving Beyond the Talk: From Difficult Dialogues to Action." In J. Armino, V. Torres, and R. Pope (eds.), *Why Aren't We There Yet: Taking Personal Responsibility for Creating an Inclusive Campus.* Washington, D.C.: Stylus Publishing, 2011.

Wijeyesinghe, C. L., Griffin, P., and Love, B. "Racism Curriculum Design." In M. Adams, L. A. Bell, and P. Griffin (eds.), *Teaching for Diversity and Social Justice.* New York: Routledge, 1997.

Zúñiga, X., Nagda, B. A., and Sevig, T. D. "Intergroup Dialogues: An Educational Model for Cultivating Engagement Across Differences." *Equity & Excellence in Education,* 2002, 35(1), 7–17.

KATHY OBEAR AND BECKY MARTINEZ *are educational consultants who worked in student affairs and are faculty members of the Social Justice Training Institute (SJTI). They facilitate race caucuses at SJTI and on college campuses. Both have published works focused on creating greater equity and inclusion on college campuses.*

9

The skill development of equanimity and empathy gained through spiritual growth equips students to examine solutions to complex problems in a diverse, global society. This chapter explores intentional multicultural initiatives designed to foster spiritual development and interfaith engagement as means to navigate difference and social good.

Spiritual Development as a Social Good

Mona Hicks, Uyen Tran-Parsons

We are each other's harvest;
We are each other's business;
We are each other's magnitude and bond.

Gwendolyn Brooks (Patel, 2007, p. 183)

The great religious diversity that exists in our communities cannot be ignored. Yet, the twenty-first-century university aims to develop global cultural competence among its students through the active search of pluralism through dialogue on religious commitments between the identities of self and others (Eck, 2006). Institutions of higher education serve as a tremendous training ground for students to learn critical thinking skills as well as develop competencies as global citizens. In the Greater Expectations National Panel Report (Association of American Colleges and Universities, 2002), the panelists call for twenty-first-century learners that are empowered, informed, and responsible with "a deeper understanding of the world they inherit, as human beings and as contributing citizens," with competency in the interconnectedness within and among global and cross-cultural communities (pp. xi–xii). Astin, Astin, and Lindholm (2011) also assert that spiritual development enhances "our sense of connectedness to one another and to the world around us" (p. 4). Through campus illustrations of the President's Interfaith and Community Service Campus Challenge that foster the balance of religious diversity and inclusion, this chapter will examine spiritual development and interfaith cooperation as a means to promote skill development to manage difference and social change.

NEW DIRECTIONS FOR STUDENT SERVICES, no. 144, Winter 2013 © 2013 Wiley Periodicals, Inc.
Published online in Wiley Online Library (wileyonlinelibrary.com) • DOI: 10.1002/ss.20072

Spiritual Development and Interfaith Cooperation

"Spirituality has to do with the values that we hold dear, our sense of who we are and where we come from, our beliefs about why we are here—the meaning and purpose that we see in our work and our life—and our sense of connectedness to one another and to the world around us" (Astin, Astin, and Lindholm, 2011, p. 4). Spiritual growth among college students enhances other college outcomes such as critical thinking and reflection to achieve agreement on matters of conscience and faith (Eck, 2006). While the degree of religious engagement somewhat declines, students grow significantly on a spiritual level and become more caring, tolerant, connected with others, and actively engaged in a spiritual quest.

Interfaith cooperation is the knowledge of how one's own faith or philosophical tradition offers an imperative for engaging with others (Patel and Meyer, 2011). Interfaith cooperation offers response to the challenge of religious diversity and builds stronger communities. It is argued that when a community engages in diverse experiences and perspectives through cooperative action, there is a significant increase in social capital (Putnam, 2007). The Harvard Pluralism Project purports that religious pluralism is the energetic engagement with diversity and the active seeking of understanding across lines of difference toward the positive end of a newly shared commitment.

President's Interfaith and Community Service Campus Challenge

In his first term, President Obama envisioned that Americans must seek ways to build communities and understanding through the contribution of a common good. He emphasized interfaith cooperation and community service, which the White House has named interfaith service. Interfaith service involves people from different religious and non-religious backgrounds tackling community challenges together. The President's Advisory Council on Faith-Based and Neighborhood Partnerships (2010), charged by the president of the United States, made recommendations on how to enact connection between the ways in which people of different faiths might work together to serve their communities. The President's Interfaith and Community Service Campus Challenge was launched in 2009, inviting colleges and universities to commit to interfaith cooperation and community service programming on campus.

In partnership with the President's Challenge, the Interfaith Youth Core (IYC) encouraged a holistic approach to modeling interfaith cooperation with the incorporation of the *Better Together* program to ensure both institutional commitment and student allies (Interfaith Youth Core, 2010). The IYC articulates the following framework as the consistent elements for best practices at institutions:

1. Use inclusive language.
2. Set and maintain safe space guidelines for dialogue and religious expression.
3. Focus on shared values, meaning-making, and self-discovery.
4. Orient around social justice and service to the community.
5. Practice storytelling as a mode for bridging religious differences.
6. Acknowledge and explore the fluidity of identity that spirituality is often a lifelong journey.
7. Keep an open invitation for community members to join in the dialogue.

These are practical skills that a campus community can foster and employ to equip students to navigate difference through greater self-awareness and greater global understanding.

Institutional Models for Spiritual Development and Interfaith Cooperation

In this section, we present two institutional models, one at a private not-for-profit university (Saint Louis University) and the other at a metropolitan public university (the University of North Texas), for spiritual development and interfaith cooperation.

Saint Louis University.   Saint Louis University (SLU) is a Jesuit, Catholic institution in an urban setting. The Jesuit, Ignatian phrase, "men and women for others," exemplifies a spiritual connection to social justice (International Centre for Jesuit Education, 1993, p. 5). Further, all Catholics are exhorted to a dialogue which will "acknowledge, preserve and promote the spiritual and moral goods found in other religions, and the values in their society and culture" in order to "join hands with them to work towards a world of peace, liberty, social justice and moral values" (The Vatican, 1965, n.n.2,3). Approximately only 40% of SLU students identify themselves a Catholic, yet the Catholic intellectual tradition inspires students to serve their communities.

The SLU program, Interfaith Challenge: Empowering Humanity through Education and Service, aims to increase awareness and participation for the many interfaith and service events occurring on campus, as well as to enhance the connection between them. In the inaugural year of the President's Interfaith and Community Service Campus Challenge, the interfaith service component of SLU's challenge consisted of four days of service (two in the fall semester and two in the spring semester): Gandhi Service Day, Make A Difference Day, Interfaith Service Saturday, and Showers of Service. Recognizing that ongoing service is what is often the most impactful, a semester-long service project was also implemented between students at SLU and children at the Youth Learning Center. Two of these projects (Gandhi Service Day and the Youth Learning Center) were funded

NEW DIRECTIONS FOR STUDENT SERVICES • DOI: 10.1002/ss

by Interfaith and Service Challenge Grants, awarded by the SLU Center for Service and Community Engagement to groups who planned events specifically for SLU's participation in the President's Interfaith and Community Service Campus Challenge. The days of service were all tremendously successful—altogether, 4,222 volunteers worked at 162 sites across the St. Louis region. Almost 4,000 of these volunteers were students. Each day had a unique interfaith aspect that enriched the service experiences of the participants. For example, Make A Difference Day began with an interfaith prayer with representatives from the Baha'i, Christian, Hindu, Jewish, and Muslim faith traditions. Later in the day, groups were given a set of questions to discuss over lunch that prompted them to reflect on how service to the community is a common thread that is woven into all faith traditions. Adding to the richness of the event was the participation of a partnership with McKendree University, the only other school in the St. Louis area to take up President Obama's Challenge. The interfaith groups from both SLU and McKendree University worked together on a neighborhood beautification project in East St. Louis, then had the opportunity to network and share ideas on how to advance interfaith initiatives on their respective campuses. The impact of these days of service was far-reaching—homes were built, schools were rehabbed, community gardens were planted, senior citizens and the disabled were visited, and meals were served to those who were hungry. Perhaps the most inspiring result from these days of service was the hope for future service efforts among SLU students. When surveyed, almost 96 percent of participants in these events were inspired to become more active in serving their community. This demonstrates that while days of service may be short in nature, the effects may have deeper connection to the understanding of how their engagement with diverse communities and religious cultures develops their ability to work within and across communities to promote social change.

As mentioned earlier, the planning committee felt that while days of service in which a broader population of the campus could come together and make a difference were important, a more small-scale, yet equally as impactful ongoing project would be important as well. The students of Interfaith and Alliance and the *Better Together* Campaign answered this call, and implemented a semester-long education seminar for the inner-city children who attend the Youth Learning Center. Inspired by the social justice mission at SLU and commitment to global citizenship, presentations were given by SLU students on various faith traditions, as well as the cultures of the people who participate in them. These sessions were given every other week during the spring semester, and contained fun and interactive activities for the youth to engage in. While it is hard to pinpoint one statistic or figure that demonstrates the impact of the interfaith service component of SLU's challenge, it perhaps can best be displayed as a measure of time.

Altogether, more than 22,000 hours of interfaith service were spent in the community of St. Louis in the 2011–2012 academic year. While not a complete measure of impact, this figure certainly displays the healthy engagement of SLU students with different belief systems and their willingness to serve and navigate those differences.

University of North Texas. The University of North Texas (UNT) is a public, metropolitan university with over 35,000 students. Spiritual life at UNT is as varied as the campus community is diverse. During the 2011–2012 academic year, the Office of Campus Life spearheaded programming initiatives to advance the interfaith engagement of students as part of the President's Interfaith and Community Service Campus Challenge. One of the most significant components of the UNT Challenge was the establishment of a Spiritual Life Council, as a dedicated group of student representatives, campus ministers, and staff members, to champion and advise the continuing development of students' spiritual examination at the University. Further, members were strategically and intentionally recruited to ensure that they represented a diverse variety of faith, tradition, and belief systems. Despite the differences in beliefs the council worked diligently and with respect for one another to enhance the educational experiences of students.

The UNT Center for Leadership and Service sponsored two large days of service during 2011–2012, with the focus of partnering interfaith organizations together in service projects. These two annual service traditions, Make a Difference Day in October 2011 and The Big Event in March 2012, had an incredible attendance and students were able to connect with one another, the campus, and the community. In addition to these programs, faith-based organizations were invited to participate in ongoing community service programs sponsored by the Center for Leadership and Service. The goal was to have service not only be for a day, but last a lifetime.

For Make a Difference Day in October, more than 750 students participated at twenty-five community partner organizations. In an effort to increase interfaith service initiatives and dialogue, Make a Difference Day intentionally matched faith-based organizations together to participate in service. The following organizations participated in Make a Difference Day 2011:

- A female Christian ministry group and mental health advocacy and education student group volunteered together at Spirit Horse, a therapeutic riding program.
- A Christian Greek fraternity and sorority along with a men's Catholic group worked together with the environmental organization, Keep Denton Beautiful.
- Latter Day Saints student organization and a Christian fraternity served together with Christian Community Action, an anti-poverty organization.

For the Big Event in March 2012, two thousand students participated at sixty-two community partner organizations. Again faith-based groups were connected with one another. At this event, all students were greeted prior to the service by a kick-off ceremony on campus and returned to campus for a celebration following the service. The following organizations participated in the Big Event 2012:

• A Jewish student organization.
• Three varied Christian student organizations.
• A mental health and advocacy group.

Students were provided reflective guidelines to discuss faith and service based on their experience. Students were asked to consider the following questions:

• In what ways are we connected by our beliefs?
• When considering our commonalities, what are the potentialities for impacting our communities?
• By articulating who we are and what we stand for, do you see an opportunity for deeper engagement and education to our communities at-large?
• How does participating in service connect with our faith beliefs? How does it connect us with others in faith discussions or of different beliefs?

In addition to these projects, more outreach has occurred to advertise service to faith-based student organizations.

Students have been given the opportunity to volunteer with ongoing and short-term projects and are encouraged to continue to be involved on campus and in the community. The impact will be more students connecting with one another and with the community as they work together to create change on the campus, in the organizations they are members, and in the broader community.

The primary evaluative efforts implemented during the inaugural challenge year at UNT involved two surveys. The first survey was distributed online to the members of the Spiritual Life Council at mid-year to capture their opinions and satisfaction of their council service experience. Key findings were that members continued to find value in their service and members continued to view the council as an important service to students. In the spring 2012 semester, a second survey was conducted through a partnership with the Spirituality Engagement Work Group affiliated with the Division of Student Affairs. A one-page spiritual climate survey was administered to students living on campus. The survey consisted of a series of demographic questions, two items regarding involvement in student religious/spiritual organizations, one item about use of the campus chapel, fifteen climate items based on the Council for the Advancement of Standards in Higher Education (CAS) standards, and two open-ended questions that allowed students to provide qualitative feedback on their perceptions of the campus climate. The response rate to the survey was approximately 8.3 percent ($n = 407$, $N = 4,889$). A basic descriptive analysis of the data revealed a generally positive experience on campus, with large percentages (75 percent and higher) of respondents reporting that they strive to connect personal values to choices, feel comfortable discussing beliefs on campus and in the classroom, and that UNT supports exploration of values and purpose. The most telling results, however, have come from a comparative analysis of participation in a religious/spiritual student organization and responses to the climate items. There were statistically significant differences on nine of the fifteen climate items. On eight of those items, revolving primarily around discussing and exploring beliefs, challenging values, and influence of values on activities and decisions, students involved in a religious/spiritual organization scored higher. Overall, it was determined that involvement in a religious/spiritual organization positively influenced students' perceptions of the campus climate, support systems, and greater understanding for diversity and complex identities of themselves and others.

Conclusion

In both private and public settings, using the simple framework aligned with the IYC *Better Together* principles, these institutions were able to facilitate measurable spiritual development and interfaith engagement as a multicultural initiative and promote change in their communities. Both institutions found that students have the capacity to interact positively through community service as well as enhance their knowledge through service learning. In addition, students gained a sense of interconnectedness through cross-cultural and interfaith cooperation as well as considered those experiences as a spiritual exercise, regardless of their religious or non-religious beliefs. Collectively, this inner and outer work, self-reflection and greater sense of connectedness, enabled students to engage with others who have different life experiences and perspectives in other aspects of their lives from a dualistic way of knowing to a pluralistic respect for others (Astin, Astin, and Lindholm, 2011).

However, since participation in service was found to be most impactful through established religious student groups, it may not be as accessible to individual students who consider themselves non-religious or have not yet developed a spiritual identity. Further, this growing population of "Nones," non-religiously affiliated students, includes a large population of diverse groups including but not limited to atheists, agnostics, seekers, secular, humanists, and those who integrate and/or identify various religious practices

(Putnam and Campbell, 2012). In January 2013, Gallup reported that 17.8 percent of the American population represents the "Nones." The Interfaith Youth Core encourages institutions both private and public to pay attention to this growing population and trends as the "Nones" do not experience the same level of comfort, engagement outside of the classroom, and perceive broad acceptance as their religious peers. Therefore, intentional efforts to diversify opportunities for discussion of different religious views among diverse populations positively affect both their spiritual development and skill development to manage difference and social change (Astin, Astin, and Lindholm, 2011).

With the rapidly changing demographic landscape in America, religion can no longer be a "taboo" topic. It has been argued that communities with greater diversity often experience great societal distance. The greater consequence of remaining religiously divided far outweighs any concerns about the separation of church and state. Individually, religion and faith are one of the most important shared characteristics among humans (Putnam, 2007). Further, the value of many faiths is the shared commonality of a commitment to community (Eck, 2006). Religious pluralism is the business of everyone in today's society and can start through the intentional work of college educators to design multicultural initiatives that foster spiritual development and interfaith cooperation to promote social good (Patel, 2007).

References

Association of American Colleges and Universities. *Greater Expectations: A New Vision for Learning as a Nation Goes to College. National Panel Report.* Washington. D.C.: Association of American Colleges and Universities, 2002.

Astin, A. W., Astin, H. S., and Lindholm, J. A. *Cultivating the Spirit: How College Can Enhance Student's Inner Lives.* San Francisco: Jossey-Bass, 2011.

Eck, D. L. *On Common Ground: World Religions in America.* New York: Columbia University Press, 2006.

Interfaith Youth Core. *Interfaith Cooperation and American Higher Education: Recommendations, Best Practices and Case Studies.* Chicago: Interfaith Youth Core, 2010.

International Centre for Jesuit Education. *Ignatian Pedagogy: A Practical Approach.* Rome, Italy: International Centre for Jesuit Education, 1993.

Patel, E. *Acts of Faith: The Story of an American Muslim, the Struggle for the Soul of a Generation.* Boston: Beacon Press, 2007.

Patel, E., and Meyer, C. "The Civic Relevance of Interfaith Cooperation for Colleges and Universities." *Journal of College & Character,* 2011, *12*(1). doi:10.2202/1940-1639.1764

President's Advisory Council on Faith-Based and Neighborhood Partnerships. *A New Era of Partnerships: Report of Recommendations to the President,* 2010. Retrieved November 15, 2012, from http://www.whitehouse.gov/sites/default/files/microsites/ofbnp-council-final-report.pdf

Putnam, R. "E Pluribus Unum: Diversity and Community in the 21st Century." *Scandinavian Political Studies,* 2007, *20*(2), 137–174.

Putnam, R., and Campbell, D. *American Grace: How Religion Divides Us and Unites Us.* New York: Simon & Schuster, 2012.

The Vatican. *Declaration on the Relation of the Church to Non-Christian Religions: Nostra Aetate,* Proclaimed by His Holiness Pope Paul VI, October 28, 1965. Rome, Italy: The Vatican.

MONA HICKS *is the assistant vice president and dean of students at Saint Louis University. She has directed transformative programs for special student populations including student athletes, veterans, and religious-affiliated groups.*

UYEN TRAN-PARSONS *works at the University of North Texas. Her work focuses on multicultural and student success initiatives.*

NEW DIRECTIONS FOR STUDENT SERVICES • DOI: 10.1002/ss

10

This chapter provides an overview of undergraduate STEM initiatives for underrepresented minorities and women, as well as a description and critical analysis of one comprehensive federally funded initiative at a research-intensive university.

Addressing Underrepresentation in STEM Fields through Undergraduate Interventions

Jodi L. Linley, Casey E. George-Jackson

Federal funding agencies, such as the National Science Foundation (NSF) and the National Institutes of Health (NIH), are invested in increasing the representation of women and people of color in science, technology, engineering, and mathematics (STEM). The U.S. Census Bureau (2008) has estimated that by 2023 more than half of all children in the United States will be children of color. In the STEM fields, three racial and ethnic groups are underrepresented: African Americans, Native Americans, and Latinos. These underrepresented minority (URM) groups comprised 12 percent of life science doctorate recipients, 10 percent of engineering doctorate recipients, and 7.8 percent of physical science doctorate recipients in 2011 (National Center for Science and Engineering Statistics [NCSES], 2011). The federal government is also concerned about women's representation in STEM fields. In 2011, women earned less than 30 percent of the doctorates in physical sciences and engineering (NCSES, 2011). U.S. population demographics, in tandem with demands for scientific and technological innovation, have led the federal government to identify increasing diversity in the STEM pipeline as a national need.

The field of student services is uniquely positioned to assist postsecondary organizations in developing effective undergraduate STEM programs to increase representation, as well as to assess and address climate

This chapter is based upon work supported by the National Science Foundation (Grant No. 0856309), the Institute of Education Sciences, U.S. Department of Education (Grant No. R305B100017 to the University of Illinois at Urbana-Champaign), and NIH-NIGMS (Grant No. 2R25GM058939). Any opinions, findings, and conclusions or recommendations expressed in this material are those of the author(s) and do not necessarily reflect the views of NSF, the Institute, the U.S. Department of Education, or NIH. The authors would also like to thank Blanca Rincon and the IBA program directors.

issues related to diversity. Unfortunately, many STEM programs focus only on increasing representation and not on the institutional issues that are barriers for many students, such as racism and sexism. A common way to redress the STEM pipeline is to create interventions at critical educational transition points, including between high school and college (Chubin, May, and Babco, 2005). STEM recruitment and retention programs exist at numerous colleges and universities across the United States and have potential for influencing the educational and career outcomes of URM and women students by providing academic advising, tutoring, and summer research opportunities (Tsui, 2007). However, programs that overlook issues of systemic oppression can be problematic, as they fail to foster long-term and enduring equitable opportunities for traditionally underrepresented students to succeed in STEM. Approaching the issue of underrepresentation and inequity in STEM in such a manner that will render intervention programs unnecessary should be a goal of institutions of higher education. However, without systemic change where cultural differences are managed, such programs and services will always be needed. Key elements of programs that do seek to address systemic oppression include emphasizing "diversity as value," grounding activities and services in theory and research, and generating support from faculty and upper-level administrators. Each of these elements is elaborated on in the following.

Philosophical Frameworks for Multicultural Initiatives

A common philosophical frame for STEM interventions, known as *teaching the exceptional and culturally different*, accepts and promotes dominant culture and curriculum by designing interventions to assist people from non-dominant groups in "catching up" (Sleeter and Grant, 2009). This framework relies on two orientations: deficiency and difference. The deficiency orientation sets low expectations for students, and cultural deficiencies are blamed when underrepresented students underachieve. The difference orientation sets high expectations and works to build students' strengths (Sleeter and Grant, 2009).

Initiatives that seek only to increase the number of URM and women students in STEM adopt the exceptional and culturally different frame, which is consistent with the concept of *diversity as good*, emphasizing surface-level outcomes (Watt, 2011). To dismantle systems of oppression and actualize the concept of *diversity as value* (Watt, 2011), STEM initiatives would need to adopt some combination of the frame described above and the multicultural social justice education frame. Such a combination would situate programs to strive for equity, confronting the reality that equal opportunity is insufficient to create equity because of institutional systems of oppression. The potential empowerment of using this framework is explored in the next section using the examples of an undergraduate STEM initiative for URM students and the results of 2009–2013 Project STEP-UP.

NEW DIRECTIONS FOR STUDENT SERVICES • DOI: 10.1002/ss

General Trends and a Program Analysis

The program analyzed in this chapter is the Iowa Biosciences Advantage (IBA), an undergraduate STEM initiative for URMs at a large, public, research-intensive, predominantly white university. National trends are drawn from Project STEP-UP, a longitudinal study on underrepresented undergraduate students in STEM fields at ten large, public, research universities. Project STEP-UP examined individual, programmatic, and institutional factors that impact students' entrance into and success in the STEM fields.

Definition of the Problem and Philosophical Frame.   It is widely accepted that efforts should be made to increase the participation of women and URM students in STEM fields. Such efforts are complicated by students often experiencing an unwelcoming climate in the STEM disciplines. URM students in STEM fields are less likely to report having a sense of belonging in their major and felt that other students in their department made them feel unwelcome (Rincon and George-Jackson, 2011). Ideally, a postsecondary organization would design and implement an undergraduate STEM initiative that both increased participation and addressed climate issues.

At its inception, IBA adopted a deficiency perspective and stressed intervention activities such as mandatory tutoring to catch URM students up with their white and Asian peers. Two years into the program's implementation, IBA leadership changed from the original principal investigators (PIs) to two new PIs. During the transition, the program underwent significant changes and shifted from a deficiency model to a difference model. Although IBA students are retained in STEM and graduate with strong applications for graduate school, the dominant culture is still promoted in STEM, and the emphasis remains on helping URM students achieve success in the existing STEM culture.

Similarly, many of the programs researched by Project STEP-UP emphasized increasing the number of undergraduate students who entered into and remained in the STEM fields. By focusing solely on the numbers, these programs tended to result in "repairing" students in order to achieve a certain outcome, such as first-to-second-year retention. Rather than taking a cultural, systemic, or institutional approach, these programs adopted a deficit-oriented approach, where students are described as "at risk" (Castro, 2012). Such programs are insufficient in addressing larger equity issues in STEM.

Program Rationale and Objectives.   When IBA was first developed, the low retention and degree completion rates for URMs in STEM departments were of central concern and were consistent with NIH's focus on improving structural diversity in STEM. The emphasis on these data allowed the involved faculty and administrators to ignore the climate issues influencing URM students' experiences in STEM. Despite this limitation, IBA is unique in that its creators utilized institutional data to respond to a call for funding rather than being based on perceptions of students' needs or by replicating other programs (George-Jackson, Castro, and Rincon, 2013).

A program's goals, objectives, and outcomes should flow directly from its rationale. For IBA, the NIH grant guidelines guided the program's goals, objectives, and outcomes. With each grant renewal, the IBA staff continuously emphasized student success and increasing structural diversity. Similar to IBA, the majority of the programs in Project STEP-UP emphasized increasing the number of students in the STEM fields, while few aimed to change the culture or climate of a particular STEM discipline.

Without proper investigation and grounding the program's rationale and objectives in theory and research, multicultural initiatives may—at best—address the symptoms of the problem rather than the problem itself. Programs that seek to repair students rather than initiate institutional change will fail to contribute to the social change that is needed to include and advance underrepresented students in the STEM fields.

Target Population.   Federal agencies have broadened their target populations to include other individuals underrepresented in STEM fields, such as students who are low income, first generation, and those with disabilities (NIH, 2013). While inclusion across all identities is laudable, developing initiatives that continue to serve underrepresented students while emphasizing a deep and broad cultural change may be more strategic. State-based bans on affirmative action complicate these efforts. Programs at public universities located in states that have banned affirmative action must balance programmatic goals that seek to provide opportunities for traditionally underrepresented students, while at the same time not deny services to other students. Some programs achieve this balance by removing eligibility requirements and opening their services to all students, allowing them to continue servicing students who will benefit most.

Activities, Assessment, and Leadership.   A program's activities should be grounded in theory and research, but when it comes to STEM diversity initiatives, the literature is sparse. Most program activities used are not empirically backed (Tsui, 2007), and programs often lack a theory of change or logic model to guide activities (George-Jackson, Castro and Rincon, 2013). Part of IBA's approach has been the reliance of the PIs on a staff director and their faculty colleagues in the College of Education, all of whom engage relevant education research, such as student development theory and institutional change theory. For example, the IBA directors collaborated with a faculty member who leads the university's Center for Evaluation and Assessment in order to develop an evaluation plan that included formative and summative assessments, a strategy that can be employed by program administrators that lack evaluation expertise (George-Jackson and Rincon, 2012).

Buy-in from faculty, staff, and upper-level administrators is critical to the long-term success of STEM intervention programs, and can be expressed in multiple ways, including providing in-kind support to the program.

Identifying appropriate faculty is a complex task, as is hiring qualified staff who are knowledgeable about the target population, available to students, and engaged in the university community. The faculty member's rank and racial identity are important considerations as well. If a junior faculty member or faculty members of color add program leadership to their portfolio, it is in their best interest to explore how that work will be valued for promotion and tenure.

Recommendations for Undergraduate STEM Diversity Initiatives

If STEM diversity initiatives seek to truly provide equitable opportunities for underrepresented students to succeed in STEM, existing programs should adopt the *diversity as value* philosophy and identify ways to address systemic oppression in STEM:

- In developing activities for undergraduate STEM diversity initiatives, *interdisciplinary research and scholarship should be incorporated* to create activities that are appropriate for the culture of each institution and meet the needs of the targeted student population. We recommend faculty and staff to consult higher education literature, such as Padilla's (1999) "black box" framework, organizational change theory, organizational culture, teaching and learning research, and stereotype management (for example, see McGee and Martin, 2011).
- Undergraduate STEM diversity initiatives should be *institution-wide initiatives*, rather than falling under one department or one administrative unit's purview. Centralized diversity initiatives can meet the needs of students within specific departments or colleges, while simultaneously encouraging cross-campus collaborations. In times of financial constraints, these collaborations allow for strategic allocation of funds. Bringing faculty and staff together increases access to resources for the students and the likelihood of institutional change.
- Measuring the efficacy of program components can be challenging, which is why we recommend working closely with a team educated and well-practiced in *evaluation research and methods*. Regardless of who designs and implements the evaluation, it is important to include formative assessment that can provide ongoing feedback to the program directors. Well-designed program evaluations also hold potential for contributing to the body of literature about undergraduate STEM diversity initiatives.
- STEM faculty play a crucial role in the experiences of undergraduate students in STEM programs. No assumptions about the multicultural competency of faculty should be made, and we recommend that any program engaging faculty should provide *resources and support for faculty development* on issues of diversity and difference.

References

Castro, E. "How We Talk about Students Matters: Reframing Deficit Discourses of Underrepresented Students in STEM." *Project STEP-UP. University of Illinois at Urbana-Champaign*, 2012. Retrieved from http://stepup.education .illinois.edu/sites/default/files/Final%20DRAFT%20-%20DAH%20-%20STEP%20UP %20Deficit%20Discourses.pdf

Chubin, D. E., May, G. S., and Babco, E. L. "Diversifying the Engineering Workforce." *Journal of Engineering Education*, 2005, *94*(1), 73–86.

George-Jackson, C. E., Castro, E., and Rincon, B. E. "What Guides the Development of STEM Intervention Programs: Examining the Role of Theories of Change." Presentation at the American Educational Research Association, San Francisco, Calif., April 27–May 1, 2013.

George-Jackson, C. E., and Rincon, B. "Increasing Sustainability of STEM Intervention Programs through Evaluation." In J. Furst-Bowe, F. Padro, and C. Veenstra (eds.), *Advancing the STEM Agenda: Quality Improvement Supports STEM*. Milwaukee: ASQ Quality Press, 2012.

McGee, E. O., and Martin, D. B. "'You Would Not Believe What I Have to Go Through to Prove My Intellectual Value!' Stereotype Management Among Academically Successful Black Mathematics and Engineering Students." *American Educational Research Journal*, 2011, *48*(6), 1347–1389.

National Center for Science and Engineering Statistics (NCSES). *Doctorate Recipients from U.S. Universities*, 2011. Retrieved February 22, 2013, from http://www.nsf .gov/statistics/sed/digest/2011/theme2.cfm#4

National Institutes of Health. *Initiative for Maximizing Student Development* (PAR-13–082), 2013. Retrieved February 22, 2013, from http://grants.nih.gov/grants /guide/pa-files/PAR-13-082.html

Padilla, R. V. "College Student Retention: Focus on Success." *Journal of College Student Retention*, 1999, *1*(2), 131–145.

Project STEP-UP, 2009–2013. University of Illinois at Urbana-Champaign. Retrieved from http://stepup.education.illinois.edu

Rincon, B., and George-Jackson, C. E. "Underrepresented Students in Science, Technology, Engineering, and Mathematics (STEM): An Examination of Campus Climate." Presentation at the American Educational Research Association, New Orleans, La., April 8–12, 2011.

Sleeter, C. E., and Grant, C. A. *Making Choices for Multicultural Education: Five Approaches to Race, Class, and Gender*. 6th ed. Hoboken, N.J.: John Wiley & Sons, 2009.

Tsui, L. "Effective Strategies to Increase Diversity in STEM Fields: A Review of the Research Literature." *The Journal of Negro Education*, 2007, *76*(4), 555–581.

U.S. Census Bureau. *An Older and More Diverse Nation by Midcentury*, 2008. Retrieved February 23, 2013, from http://www.census.gov/newsroom/releases/archives /population/cb08-123.html

Watt, S. K. "Moving Beyond the Talk: From Difficult Dialogues to Action." In J. Armino, V. Torres, and R. Pope (eds.), *Why Aren't We There Yet: Taking Personal Responsibility for Creating an Inclusive Campus*. Sterling, Va.: Stylus Publishing, 2011.

JODI L. LINLEY *is a doctoral student of higher, adult, and lifelong education at Michigan State University, with a longstanding career and research agenda centered on issues of equity and multiculturalism.*

CASEY E. GEORGE-JACKSON *is an IES postdoctoral fellow in Mathematics Education Research at the University of Illinois at Urbana-Champaign.*

NEW DIRECTIONS FOR STUDENT SERVICES • DOI: 10.1002/ss

Index

suicide prevention that addresses both at-risk groups and the general campus population. Since 2005, 138 colleges and universities have received funding under the Garrett Lee Smith Memorial Act to develop and implement campus suicide prevention programs. This volume of *New Directions for Student Services* highlights successful strategies implemented by grantee campuses. We hope these approaches can serve as models to address student suicide on other campuses.
ISBN 978-11186-94831

SS140   **Developing Students Leadership Capacity**
Kathy L. Guthrie, Laura Osteen, Editors
Leadership education has become an essential outcome of higher education in the past decade and yet leadership development efforts vary greatly on campuses. While some efforts are centralized, most are decentralized and lack campus-wide coordination. Leadership educators have sought out associations and other professional networks to increase their capacity to develop, implement, and assess leadership development opportunities.

In response to the increase accreditation movement, the International Leadership Association (ILA) published "Guiding Questions: Guidelines for Leadership Education Programs." The Guiding Questions document is a result of a five-year, collaborative process to create guidelines for leadership education programs. ILA's format of open-ended guiding questions is applicable to any student affairs practitioner developing a leadership learning program. This sourcebook was developed specifically to assist higher education professionals in their understanding, conceptualization, and implementation of the five standards outlined in the ILA Guiding Questions: Context, Conceptual Framework, Content, Teaching and Learning, and Assessment of Leadership Education.

The purpose of this *New Directions for Student Services* sourcebook is to explore leadership education for undergraduate students and provide a foundation for readers to develop students' leadership capacity. Using the ILA's Guiding Questions as a framework, this sourcebook will present an approach to the development of leadership education programs.
ISBN 978-11185-40909

SS139   **Facilitating the Moral Growth of College Students**
Debora L. Liddell, Diane L. Cooper, Editors
Moral development is a powerful task of young adulthood, and attending to that development is a mandate expected of institutions of higher education. Liddell and Cooper offer a practical approach to understanding how moral learning occurs as well as the role of mentors and educators in facilitating that learning. Using Rest's Four Component Model—moral sensitivity, judgment, motivation, and action—they describe powerful campus initiatives for moral growth, including service-learning, civic engagement, campus judicial systems, diversity and social justice initiatives, and sustainability efforts. Guidelines for effective moral mentorship are examined, and assessment approaches are described in some detail.
ISBN 978-11184-70909

SS138 *Stepping Up to Stepping Out: Helping Students Prepare for Life After College*
George S. McClellan, Jill Parker, Editors
Undergraduate students come to college from a myriad of pathways for a variety of purposes, and the same can be said of them as they leave to head off into their next endeavors. Arguably, the most important goal of higher education is to prepare students to achieve their post-college aspirations, and campuses typically pursue that goal through a combination of curricular and co-curricular programs and services for students. This manuscript offers readers a glimpse into contemporary context and practice related to helping students with their after-college transition from one form of education (two-year or four-year) to the next (four-year, graduate, or professional school), from education to workforce, or from education to military service.
ISBN 978-11184-43972

SS137 *Enhancing Sustainability Campuswide*
Bruce A. Jacobs, Jillian Kinzie, Editors
"Do what you can, with what you have, where you are." This bit of homespun philosophy aptly describes the practice of many student affairs professionals. It's a useful guide for educators who believe in the value of teaching and learning in every personal interaction. As resources are stretched and the challenges facing our students and institutions grow, this approach can help make sustainability a focus for planning and implementation across the breadth of student affairs programs. Many student affairs divisions are doing just that, leading the way in sustainability education by providing students with the knowledge they need to make a positive impact in their personal, civic, and professional lives.

This sourcebook provides a primer on how to best organize specific programs and services as well as overall campus operations to address the critical challenge of sustainability. The authors present research, operational approaches, and personal insights to enable readers to develop successful programs and services. The intent is to offer material that can be adapted into existing or developing programs for a seamless integration of sustainability into everyday campus life.
ISBN 978-11183-45801

SS136 *Supporting and Supervising Mid-Level Professionals*
Larry D. Roper, Editor
Mid-level professionals promoted to a supervisory role often find themselves in a novel position—attending to their own professional growth and career development while having to nurture the performance and success of others. In many cases, newly promoted supervisors are still cultivating their professional identity and mastering the challenges of a more complex role as they are learning to supervise other early career professionals, office staff, graduate students, or undergraduates. Stress and anxiety naturally accompany the demands of such a job, particularly in the academic world, an environment that can require sensitivity to multicultural issues, supervision by virtual means, and navigation of an occasionally difficult, opaque hierarchy.

The authors of this sourcebook blend research, personal essays, case studies, and their personal experiences to illuminate the needs and challenges of midlevel supervisors. It is the editor's hope that the perspectives and stories offered here will help all student services professionals trying to grow into new positions of responsibility.
ISBN 978-11182-31456

SS135   ***Advancing the Integrity of Professional Practice***
Robert B. Young, Editor
Integrity is more than a proclamation in mission statements or a component of leadership training. Integrity is, as well, a test offered at any hour. Passing it is seldom rewarded, but failing it can ruin lives. Student affairs administrators must know what integrity requires in all its forms if they want to protect and expand the worth of higher education. Readers of this volume will learn how integrity affects the trustworthiness of their organizations and operations. They will have the opportunity to read about the highest goals and the best practices of leadership, as well as some practical strategies that can help them deal with challenges to organizational and individual integrity.
ISBN 978-11181-51167

SS134   ***Fostering the Increased Integration of Students with Disabilities***
Marianne S. Huger, Editor
This volume addresses higher education administrators and college professors beyond those working in the area of disability services. All members of a community benefit from the diversity that students with disabilities bring to a campus. At the same time, all campus constituents have an obligation to serve the diverse students that are present on their campuses. Therefore, all members must have the knowledge and professional preparation to navigate issues surrounding the increased integration of students with disabilities. This volume provides that preparation and knowledge by addressing questions ranging from design—of both facilities and online material—and transition services to education abroad, psychiatric support, and legal issues.

By framing access to higher education within a contextual goal of increasing the social and academic integration of students with disabilities, the authors aim to provide practitioners and faculty members with guidance that goes beyond accommodation to including students in the fabric of their institution.
ISBN 978-11180-95119

NEW DIRECTIONS FOR STUDENT SERVICES

ORDER FORM SUBSCRIPTION AND SINGLE ISSUES

DISCOUNTED BACK ISSUES:

Use this form to receive 20% off all back issues of *New Directions for Student Services*.
All single issues priced at **$23.20** (normally $29.00)

TITLE	ISSUE NO.	ISBN

*Call 888-378-2537 or see mailing instructions below. When calling, mention the promotional code JBNND
to receive your discount. For a complete list of issues, please visit www.josseybass.com/go/ndss*

SUBSCRIPTIONS: (1 YEAR, 4 ISSUES)

☐ New Order   ☐ Renewal

U.S.	☐ Individual: $89	☐ Institutional: $311
CANADA/MEXICO	☐ Individual: $89	☐ Institutional: $351
ALL OTHERS	☐ Individual: $113	☐ Institutional: $385

*Call 888-378-2537 or see mailing and pricing instructions below.
Online subscriptions are available at www.onlinelibrary.wiley.com*

ORDER TOTALS:

Issue / Subscription Amount: $ _____

Shipping Amount: $ _____
(for single issues only – subscription prices include shipping)

Total Amount: $ _____

SHIPPING CHARGES:

First Item	$6.00
Each Add'l Item	$2.00

*(No sales tax for U.S. subscriptions. Canadian residents, add GST for subscription orders. Individual rate subscriptions must
be paid by personal check or credit card. Individual rate subscriptions may not be resold as library copies.)*

BILLING & SHIPPING INFORMATION:

☐ **PAYMENT ENCLOSED:** *(U.S. check or money order only. All payments must be in U.S. dollars.)*

☐ **CREDIT CARD:**   ☐ VISA   ☐ MC   ☐ AMEX

Card number _____Exp. Date_____

Card Holder Name_____Card Issue # _____

Signature _____Day Phone _____

☐ **BILL ME:** *(U.S. institutional orders only. Purchase order required.)*

Purchase order # _____
Federal Tax ID 13559302 • GST 89102-8052

Name_____

Address_____

Phone_____ E-mail_____

Copy or detach page and send to: **John Wiley & Sons, One Montgomery Street, Suite 1200,
San Francisco, CA 94104-4594**

Order Form can also be faxed to: **888-481-2665**

PROMO JBNND

Statement of Ownership

Statement of Ownership, Management, and Circulation (required by 39 U.S.C. 3685), filed on OCTOBER 1, 2013 for NEW DIRECTIONS FOR STUDENT SERVICES (Publication No. 0164-7970), published Quarterly for an annual subscription price of $89 at Wiley Subscription Services, Inc., at Jossey-Bass, One Montgomery St., Suite 1200, San Francisco, CA 94104-4594.

The names and complete mailing addresses of the Publisher, Editor, and Managing Editor are: Publisher, Wiley Subscription Services, Inc., A Wiley Company at San Francisco, One Montgomery St., Suite 1200, San Francisco, CA 94104-4594; Editor, Elizabeth J. Whitt, Editor in Chief, 221 North Grand, DuBourg Hall, Room 455, Saint Louis University, St. Louis, MO 63103; Managing Editor, John Schuh, Assoc.Editor, 1706 Amherst Drive, Ames, IA 50014. Contact Person: Joe Schuman; Telephone: 415-782-3232.

NEW DIRECTIONS FOR STUDENT SERVICES is a publication owned by Wiley Subscription Services, Inc., 111 River St., Hoboken, NJ 07030. The known bondholders, mortgages, and other security holders owning or holding 1% or more of total amount of bonds, mortgages, or other securities are (see list).

	Average No. Copies Each Issue During Preceding 12 Months	No. Copies of Single Issue Published Nearest To Filing Date (Summer 2013)
15a. Total number of copies (net press run)	667	542
15b. Legitimate paid and/or requested distribution (by mail and outside mail)		
15b(1). Individual paid/requested mail subscriptions stated on PS form 3541 (include direct written request from recipient, telemarketing, and Internet requests from recipient, paid subscriptions including nominal rate subscriptions, advertiser's proof copies, and exchange copies)	197	205
15b(2). Copies requested by employers for distribution to employees by name or position, stated on PS form 3541	0	0
15b(3). Sales through dealers and carriers, street vendors, counter sales, and other paid or requested distribution outside USPS	0	0
15b(4). Requested copies distributed by other mail classes through USPS	0	0
15c. Total paid and/or requested circulation (sum of 15b(1), (2), (3), and (4))	197	205
15d. Nonrequested distribution (by mail and outside mail)		
15d(1). Outside county nonrequested copies stated on PS form 3541	37	36
15d(2). In-county nonrequested copies stated on PS form 3541	0	0
15d(3). Nonrequested copies distributed through the USPS by other classes of mail	0	0
15d(4). Nonrequested copies distributed outside the mail	0	0
15e. Total nonrequested distribution (sum of 15d(1), (2), (3), and (4))	37	36
15f. Total distribution (sum of 15c and 15e)	234	241
15g. Copies not distributed	433	301
15h. Total (sum of 15f and 15g)	667	542
15i. Percent paid and/or requested circulation (15c divided by 15f times 100)	84.8%	85%

I certify that all information furnished on this form is true and complete. I understand that anyone who furnishes false or misleading information on this form or who omits material or information requested on this form may be subject to criminal sanctions (including fines and imprisonment) and/or civil sanctions (including civil penalties).

Statement of Ownership will be printed in the Winter 2013 issue of this publication.

(signed) Susan E. Lewis, VP & Publisher-Periodicals